GW00568211

SPINNING

by Deirdre Kinahan

Fishamble is funded by the Arts Council,
Dublin City Council and Culture Ireland

Baile Átha Cliath
Dublin City

Culture Ireland
Cultúr Éireann

Spinning by Deirdre Kinahan was first produced by
Fishamble: The New Play Company in Smock Alley Theatre,
as part of Dublin Theatre Festival, on 3 October 2014 with
the following cast and production team.

Cast

Conor	Karl Shiels
Susan	Fiona Bell
Jen	Janet Moran
Annie	Caitriona Ennis

Production Team

Director	Jim Culleton
Producer	Marketa Dowling
Set Designer	Sabine Dargent
Lighting Designer	Kevin Smith
Costume Designer	Léonore McDonagh
Sound Designer	Denis Clohessy
Graphic Designer	Ronan Nulty & Dan O'Neill at Publicis
Dramaturg	Gavin Kostick
Production Manager	Tom Dowling
Stage Manager	Stephanie Ryan
Assistant Stage Manager	Sarah Maloney
PR	Sinead O'Doherty at Gerry Lundberg PR
Stills Photographer	Pat Redmond
Video Promotion	Evan Flynn
Production Assistant	Andrea Cleary
Dialect Adviser	Anthony Morris
Assistant Director	Colette Cullen *
Assistant LX/LX Operator	Shane McGill
Set Design Intern	Rachel Kearns **
Cover Photo	Leo Byrne

*Placement as part of Fishamble's theatre company-in-association
status at UCD

** Placement from The Lir Academy

The production runs for 80 minutes without an interval.

About Fishamble: The New Play Company

Fishamble is an award-winning, internationally acclaimed Irish theatre company, dedicated to the discovery, development and production of new work. So far, it has produced 136 new plays, including 47 stand-alone plays and 89 short plays as part of longer works, by first-time and established playwrights.

Fishamble is committed to touring throughout Ireland and internationally, and typically presents over 200 performances of its plays in approximately 80 venues per year. Fishamble has earned a reputation as 'a global brand with international theatrical presence' (*Irish Times*), 'forward-thinking Fishamble' (*New York Times*) and 'Ireland's excellent Fishamble' (*Guardian*) through touring its productions to audiences in Ireland as well as to England, Scotland, Wales, France, Germany, Iceland, Croatia, Belgium, Czech Republic, Switzerland, Bulgaria, Romania, Serbia, Turkey, USA, Canada and Australia.

Awards for Fishamble productions include Fringe First, Herald Angel, Argus Angel, MAMCA, 1st Irish and Irish Times Theatre Awards. Many of its first-time playwrights have won Stewart Parker Trust Awards. During 2013, to celebrate the company's 25th birthday, Fishamble donated its living archive to the National Library of Ireland.

Fishamble is at the heart of new writing for theatre in Ireland, not just through its productions, but through its extensive programme of Training, Development and Mentoring schemes. Each year, Fishamble supports 60% of the writers of all new plays produced on the island of Ireland, approximately 50 plays per year. This happens in a variety of ways; for instance, Fishamble supports:

• **the public** through an ongoing range of playwriting courses in Dublin and off-site for literary and arts festivals nationwide

• **playwrights and theatre companies** through *The New Play Clinic*, which develops new plays planned for production by theatre artists and companies, and the annual *Fishamble New Writing Award* at Dublin Fringe

• **actors** through its *Show in a Bag* programme, which creates and showcases new plays for actors, in association with the Irish Theatre Institute and Dublin Fringe

• **students** through work in association with TCD, NUIG, NUIM, IES, DIT, and as *Theatre Company in Association* at UCD Drama Studies Centre

• **emerging artists** through *Mentoring Schemes* in association with venues and local authorities, for playwrights and directors.

'Fishamble puts electricity in the National grid of dreams'
Sebastian Barry

'Without Fishamble, Irish theatre would be anaemic.' **Brian Friel**

Fishamble: The New Play Company
Shamrock Chambers
1/2 Eustace Street
Dublin 2
Ireland
Tel: +353–1–670 4018,
fax: +353–1–670 4019

email: info@fishamble.com
www.fishamble.com
www.facebook.com/fishamble
www.twitter.com/fishamble

Previous Fishamble World Premiere Productions

2014
Little Thing, Big Thing by
Donal O'Kelly
Swing by Steve Blount*,
Peter Daly*, Gavin Kostick and
Janet Moran*
Guaranteed! by Colin Murphy
(revival)
Silent by Pat Kinevane (revival)
Forgotten by Pat Kinevane
(revival)

2013
The Bruising of Clouds by Sean
McLoughlin (now Sean P Maguire)
Guaranteed! by Colin Murphy*
Tiny Plays for Ireland 2 by 25 writers
Silent by Pat Kinevane (revival)
The Great Goat Bubble by
Julian Gough (revival)
The Wheelchair on My Face by
Sonya Kelly (revival)
Forgotten by Pat Kinevane
(revival)

2012
Tiny Plays for Ireland by 25 writers
Silent by Pat Kinevane (revival)
The Great Goat Bubble by
Julian Gough*
The Wheelchair on My Face by
Sonya Kelly*
Forgotten by Pat Kinevane
(revival)

2011
Silent by Pat Kinevane
The End of the Road by
Gavin Kostick
The Pride of Parnell Street by
Sebastian Barry (revival)
Forgotten by Pat Kinevane
(revival)
The Music of Ghost Light by
Joseph O'Connor
Noah and the Tower Flower by
Sean McLoughlin (revival)

2010
Big Ole Piece of Cake by
Sean McLoughlin
Turning Point by John Austin
Connolly, Steve Daunt*,
Stephen Kennedy,
Rosaleen McDonagh
Forgotten (revival) by
Pat Kinevane

2009
Strandline by Abbie Spallen
The Pride of Parnell Street by
Sebastian Barry (revival)
Forgotten by Pat Kinevane
(revival)
Handel's Crossing by
Joseph O'Connor
Noah and the Tower Flower by
Sean McLoughlin (revival)

2008
Forgotten by Pat Kinevane
(revival)
The Pride of Parnell Street by
Sebastian Barry (revival)
Rank by Robert Massey

2007
The Pride of Parnell Street by
Sebastian Barry
Noah and the Tower Flower by
Sean McLoughlin*
Forgotten by Pat Kinevane

2006
Monged by Gary Duggan (revival)
Whereabouts – a series of short,
site-specific plays by Shane Carr*,
John Cronin*, John Grogan*,
Louise Lowe, Belinda McKeon*,
Colin Murphy*, Anna Newell*,
Jack Olohan*, Jody O'Neill*, Tom
Swift and Jacqueline Strawbridge*
The Gist of It by Rodney Lee*

2005
Monged by Gary Duggan*
She Was Wearing... by Sebastian
Barry, Maeve Binchy, Dermot
Bolger, Michael Collins,
Stella Feehily, Rosalind Haslett,
Róisín Ingle*, Marian Keyes* and
Gavin Kostick

2004
Pilgrims in the Park by
Jim O'Hanlon
Tadhg Stray Wandered In by
Michael Collins

2003

Handel's Crossing by Joseph O'Connor, *The Medusa* by Gavin Kostick, *Chaste Diana* by Michael West and *Sweet Bitter* by Stella Feehily (a season of radio plays) *Shorts* by Dawn Bradfield*, Aino Dubrawsky*, Simon O'Gorman*, Ciara Considine*, Tina Reilly*, Mary Portser, Colm Maher*, James Heaney*, Tara Dairman*, Lorraine McArdle*, Talaya Delaney*, Ger Gleeson*, Stella Feehily* and Bryan Delaney* *The Buddhist of Castleknock* by Jim O'Hanlon (revival)

2002

Contact by Jeff Pitcher and Gavin Kostick
The Buddhist of Castleknock by Jim O'Hanlon*
Still by Rosalind Haslett*

2001

The Carnival King by Ian Kilroy*
Wired to the Moon by Maeve Binchy, adapted by Jim Culleton

2000

Y2K Festival: Consenting Adults by Dermot Bolger, *Dreamframe* by Deirdre Hines, *Moonlight and Music* by Jennifer Johnston, *The Great Jubilee* by Nicholas Kelly*, *Doom Raider* by Gavin Kostick, *Tea Set* by Gina Moxley

1999

The Plains of Enna by Pat Kinevane
True Believers by Joseph O'Connor

1998

The Nun's Wood by Pat Kinevane*

1997

From Both Hips by Mark O'Rowe*

1996

The Flesh Addict by Gavin Kostick

1995

Sardines by Michael West
Red Roses and Petrol by Joseph O'Connor*

1994

Jack Ketch's Gallows Jig by Gavin Kostick

1993

Buffalo Bill Has Gone To Alaska by Colin Teevan
The Ash Fire by Gavin Kostick (revival)

1992

The Ash Fire by Gavin Kostick*
The Tender Trap by Michael West

1991

Howling Moons/Silent Sons by Deirdre Hines*
This Love Thing by Marina Carr

1990

Don Juan by Michael West

* denotes first play by a new playwright as part of *Fishamble Firsts*

New plays are under commission from Sebastian Barry, Gavin Kostick, Pat Kinevane, Darren Donohue, Colin Murphy and Rosaleen McDonagh as well as a new project-in-development with Crash Ensemble and CoisCéim.

Fishamble Staff

Artistic Director   Jim Culleton
General Manager   Marketa Dowling
Literary Manager   Gavin Kostick
Production Assistant   Andrea Cleary

Fishamble Board

Tania Banotti, Padraig Burns, Caroline Cullen, Peter Finnegan, Liz Nugent, Vincent O'Doherty, Andrew Parkes (Chair).

Thanks

Fishamble wishes to thank the following Friends of Fishamble for their invaluable support: Alan and Rosemarie Ashe, Mary Banotti, Tania Banotti, Padraig Burns, Caroilin Callery, Maura Connolly, John Fanagan, Barbara FitzGerald, Brian Friel, Pauline Gibney, Katharyn Given, Ann Glynn, Alan & Caroline Gray, Eithne Healy, Georganne Aldrich Heller, Gillie Hinds, Jane and Geoffrey Keating, Brenda Kent, Malcolm Kindness, Lisney, Richard McCullough, Patrick Molloy, Pat Moylan, Aidan Murphy, Colin Murphy, Dympna Murray, Padraig Naughton, Liz Nugent, Lucy Nugent, Michael O'Connor, Vincent O'Doherty, Joanna Parkes, Nancy Pasley, Grace Perrott, David and Veronica Rowe, Mark Ryan, Colleen Savage, Mary Sheerin, Grace Smith, Patrick and Mo Sutton. Thank you to all who do not wish to be credited.

Special thanks to: David Parnell, Maeve Giles and all at the Arts Council; Ray Yeates and all at Dublin City Council Arts Office; Willie White and all at Dublin Theatre Festival, and all those who have helped Fishamble with the production since this publication went to print.

Biographies

DEIRDRE KINAHAN (Writer)

Deirdre is actively involved in the Irish Theatre Sector both as Playwright and Producer. She was a founding member and Artistic Director of Tall Tales Theatre Company for 15 years and now sits on the Stewart Parker Trust advisory board, whose mission is to encourage new writing for the stage. Deirdre sits on the board of the Abbey Theatre and Theatre Forum Ireland. Her work is translated into many languages and produced regularly both in Ireland and on the international stage. She is currently under commission to Manhattan Theatre Club, New York, with a further play in development in the UK. Her play *God's Hotel* will receive a Dublin premiere in 2015 with the support of the Jim McNaughton Tilestyle Bursary, Project Arts Centre, Solstice Arts Centre, Meath County Council and Irish Theatre Institute. Deirdre is co-writing her first feature film with the support of the Irish Film Board and has another feature in development with BLINDER films, Dublin. She is published by Nick Hern Books. Deirdre wrote *PROTEST* for the Royal Court (London) Open Season 2013 and her most recent play *These Halcyon Days* played at Dublin Theatre Festival in 2012 before touring to New York and winning a Fringe First at the Edinburgh Festival 2013 with Landmark Productions. *These Halcyon Days* was also nominated as best play by the Irish Times Theatre Awards 2012. Her play *MOMENT* was a major hit at the Bush Theatre in 2011 and in Chicago in 2012. *Hue & Cry* and *BOGBOY* have won critical acclaim at the First Irish Festival in New York, winning three awards and Critics' Pick in the *New York Times*. Deirdre has received many awards and bursaries, including the Tony Doyle Award, BBC Northern Ireland in 2009, Peggy Ramsay Trust Award 2014 and is currently the recipient of the Jim McNaughton TileSytle Bursary from Business to Arts, Ireland. Her debut play for BBC Radio 4 *A Bag on Ballyfinch Place* aired in January and won Critics' Choice in the *Observer*, *Telegraph* and *Radio Times*. Writing for theatre includes: *SPINNING* (Fishamble: The New Play Company, Dublin Theatre Festival 2014); *PROTEST* (Royal Court Theatre, London, PIIGS Project 2013); *THESE HALCYON DAYS* (Dublin Theatre Festival/New York/Edinburgh 2012/13); *BROKEN* (Fishamble, Tiny Plays for Ireland, Dublin 2012); *Transgressor, Where's My Seat* (Bush, London, 2011); *BOGBOY* (Tall Tales and Solstice Arts Centre, New York and national tour); *MOMENT* (Tall Tales and Solstice Arts Centre, Bush and national tour); *SALAD DAY* (Abbey); *HUE & CRY* (Bewley's Café and Tall Tales, Glasgow, Romania, Bulgaria, Paris and New York); *MELODY* (Tall Tales, Glasgow, national tour); *ATTABOY MR SYNGE* (The Civic Theatre national tour); *RUM & RAISIN* (Tall Tales and Nogin Theatre Co. national tour); *SUMMER FRUITS* (Tall Tales, national tour); *KNOCKNASHEE* (Tall Tales and The Civic Theatre, national tour); *PASSAGE* (Tall Tales, The Civic Theatre); *BÉ CARNA* (Tall Tales, national tour and Edinburgh Festival Fringe).

For children; *Maisy Daly's Rainbow* (Tall Tales and Solstice); *Rebecca's Robin* (Bewley's Café); *Show Child* (Livin Dred); *The Tale of the Blue Eyed Cat* (Livin' Dred).

For radio: *BOGBOY, A BAG ON BALLYFINCH PLACE.* Adaptations: Deirdre works regularly with Meath County Council Arts Office as mentor and playwright. She has recently adapted the superb writings of Mary Lavin for the stage.

KARL SHIELS (Performer: Conor)

Karl previously worked with Fishamble: The New Play Company in *The Pride of Parnell Street* by Sebastian Barry. Karl is Artistic Director of Theatre Upstairs @ Lanigan's Bar, Dublin, and was awarded the 2013 Irish Times Special Judges' Award in recognition of his contribution to Irish theatre in that venue. As an actor, theatre credits include: *Beauty in a Broken Place*, *At Swim-Two Birds*, *The Barbaric Comedies*, *Twenty Grand*, *Henry IV (Part 1)*, *Romeo and Juliet*, *Terminus*, *The Comedy of Errors*, *Macbeth*, *The Resistible Rise of Arturo Ui*, *The House*, *Drumbelly* (all for the Abbey and Peacock); *Howie the Rookie* (Bush/Peacock/international tour); *The Shadow of a Gunman* (Lyric, Belfast); *Duck* (Out of Joint/Royal Court); *Oedipus Loves You* (Pan Pan); *The Death of Harry Leon* (Ouroboros; nominated for an Irish Times Award for Best Supporting Actor 2009); *Comedians* (Bickerstaffe; winner of Best Actor Award at the Dublin Theatre Festival 1999); *Penelope* (Druid; nominated for a Best Actor Award in 2010 Stage Awards and an Irish Times Theatre Awards, Best Actor Award in 2011). Television credits include: *The Clinic* (RTÉ); *Doctors* (BBC); *Any Time Now* (BBCNI/RTÉ); *Attachments* (BBC2); *On Home Ground* (RTÉ); *Foyle's War* (UTV); *Undeniable* (UTV); *The Tudors* (HBO); *Prosperity* (RTÉ); *Peaky Blinders* (BBC); *The Walshes* (BBC/RTÉ); *Titanic: Blood and Steel* (DAP); *Camera Café* (RTÉ). Film credits include: *Batman Begins*, *Veronica Guerin*, *Intermission*, *Mystics*, *Meeting Che Guevara & the Man from Maybury Hill*, *Trafficked* – IFTA Best Actor nomination, *Haywire*, *Savage*, *The Hard Way*, *Davin*, *Jack Taylor*, *Angel*, *Butchers*, *No Justice*, *Death's Door*, *Eden*, *Waiting for Dublin*, *W.C.*, *Virtues of a Sinner*, *Freaky Deaky 10 to 1*, *Clubbing*, *Between Dreams*, *Stitches*, *Shadow Dancer*, *Wild* and *Noble*. Karl is currently playing Robbie Quinn in *Fair City* for RTÉ.

FIONA BELL (Performer: Susan)

Fiona previously played Máirín in *Strandline* by Abbie Spallen, produced by Fishamble: The New Play Company. Other theatre credits include: *The Price*, *The Vortex*, *An Enemy of the People*, *Jane Eyre*, *Boston Marriage*, *Les Liaisons Dangereuses*, *Present Laughter* (transfer to Spoleto Festival), *The Real Thing*, *Pride and Prejudice*, *See you Next Tuesday* (all at the Gate); *Major Barbara*, *Pygmalion*, *The Dead*, *Only an Apple*, *Three Sisters*, *A Month in the Country*, *Medea* (Abbey); *Further than the Furthest Thing*, *The Country* (Hatch Theatre Co. in association with The Project Theatre); *Leaves* (Druid); *How Many Miles to Babylon* (Second Age); *Dinner with Friends* (Gúna Nua and Andrew's Lane); *Henry VI, Parts 1, 2 and 3*, *Richard III* (Royal Shakespeare Company); *Snake* (Hampstead, London); *Animal* (Soho, London); *Adrenalin Heart* (Bush, London); *The Misanthrope* (Chichester); *Dancing at Lughnasa*, *Mirandolina*, *Oleanna*, *Bedroom Farce*, *The Master Builder* (Royal Lyceum, Edinburgh); *Macbeth*, *Good*, *Cinderella*, *Brilliant Traces*, *Mate in Three* (Tron, Glasgow), *The Lament for Arthur Cleary*, *Jump the Life to Come*, *Vodka and Daisies* (7:84 Theatre Co, Glasgow). Film/television credits include: *Loving Miss Hatto*, *A Low Winter Sun*, *Taggart*, *Casualty*, *Maneaters*, *The Creatives*, *City Central*, *The Bill*, *EastEnders*, *Rockface*, *The Eustace Brothers*, *Doctors*, *Soldier Soldier*, *Trainspotting*, *Gregory's 2 Girls*, *I Saw You*, *Afterlife*, *Mistgate*, *Between Dreams*, *Stand and Deliver*, *Duck*, *Truth or Dare*.

JANET MORAN (Performer: Jen)

Most recently Janet Moran performed in *Swing*, which she also co-wrote, produced by Fishamble: The New Play Company (New York, Paris, Edinburgh Festival Fringe and national tour). Janet's other stage work includes *Juno and the Paycock* (National Theatre, London/Abbey Theatre co-production); *Shibari, Translations, No Romance, The Recruiting Officer, The Cherry Orchard, She Stoops to Conquer, Communion, The Barbaric Comedies, The Well of the Saints* and *The Hostage* (all at the Abbey); *The Bridge Below the Town* (Livin' Dred); *Car Show, Dublin by Lamplight, Everyday, Freefall* and *Desire Under The Elms* (The Corn Exchange); *Dead Funny* (Rough Magic); *Stella by Starlight* (Gate); *Romeo and Juliet, Othello* (Second Age). Other theatre credits include: *Pineapple, Xaviers, Royal Supreme, Her Big Chance, Unravelling the Ribbon, Dancing at Lughnasa, Playing from the Heart, Guess Who's Coming to Dinner, All's Well That Ends Well, Emma, The Rep Experiment* and *The Stomping Ground*. Film/television credits include: *Trivia, Love/Hate, Love is the Drug, The Clinic* and *The Savage Eye* (RTÉ); *The Butcher Boy, Breakfast on Pluto, Milo, Minim Rest, Bono and My Ex, Moll Flanders, Nothing Personal, Volkswagen Joe* and *Quirke* (BBC).

CAITRIONA ENNIS (Performer: Annie)

This is Caitriona's first time working with Fishamble: The New Play Company. Caitriona attended University College Dublin, where she completed a BA in English and Drama, served as Auditor of UCD Dramsoc (2010/2011) and completed her MA in Drama and Performance. During her time in UCD, she was awarded the Patrick Semple Medal for outstanding academic achievement in Drama Studies, as well as the UCD President's Award. In 2011 she was awarded the Ad Astra Academy scholarship for Drama. Caitriona's theatre credits include: *A Whistle in the Dark* (ISDA Award for Best Actress 2011); her work with ANU Productions includes *Taking to the Bed* (Phizz Fest); *The Boys of Foley Street* (Dublin Theatre Festival 2012, nominated for Best Actress in the Irish Times Theatre Awards 2013); *THIRTEEN* (nominated for a Best Actress Dublin Fringe Award 2013) and she has just finished a run with ANU's *Angel Meadow* in Manchester. Other credits include Joan in *The Lark* (Fast Intent, Smock Alley); Ciara in *NARF* by Caitriona Daly, *Text Messages* (Project Arts Centre); *The State Commemoration* (ANU Productions); *Annabelle's Star* by Raymond Keane and Mary McNally (The Ark) and *The Ugly One* (The Lir Academy).

JIM CULLETON (Director)

Jim Culleton is artistic director of Fishamble: The New Play Company for which he has directed productions that have toured throughout Ireland, UK, US, Canada, Australia and 12 European countries, and have won awards including Fringe First, Herald Angel, Argus Angel, 1st Irish, MAMCA and Irish Times Theatre Awards. Most recent productions for Fishamble are *Little Thing, Big Thing* by Donal O'Kelly, *Tiny Plays for Ireland 1 & 2* by 50 writers, *Silent* and *Forgotten* by Pat Kinevane, *The Pride of Parnell Street* by Sebastian Barry, *The Bruising of Clouds* and *Noah and the Tower Flower* by Sean P Maguire, *The Music of Ghost Light* by Joseph O'Connor, and *Turning Point* in association with ADI/VSA/ Kennedy Center. He has also directed for the Abbey, most recently *Down Off His Stilts* (Dublin, Sligo, Boston), *Bookworms* by Bernard Farrell and *Shush* by Elaine Murphy, as well as for 7:84 (Scotland), Project Arts Centre, Amharclann de híde, Amnesty International, Tinderbox, The Passion Machine, The Ark, Second Age, RTÉ Radio, the Belgrade, TNL Canada, Scotland's Ensemble @ Dundee Rep, Draíocht, Barnstorm, Roundabout, TCD School of Drama, Guna Nua, RTÉ lyric fm, Frontline Defenders, Irish Council for Bioethics, Origin (New York) and Woodpecker Productions/Gaiety. He is Adjunct Lecturer at TCD, and has taught for Notre Dame, NYU, The Lir, NUIM/GSA, and UCD, where Fishamble is theatre company-in-association. Current projects include a range of Fishamble training, mentoring and development initiatives, and he will next direct Fishamble's *Underneath* by Pat Kinevane as part of Limerick City of Culture.

MARKETA DOWLING (Producer)

Marketa is the General Manager and Producer of Fishamble: The New Play Company for which she has most recently produced *Swing* by Steve Blount, Peter Daly, Gavin Kostick and Janet Moran (Irish tour and New York, Paris and Edinburgh), *Little Thing, Big Thing* by Donal O'Kelly, *Guaranteed!* (Irish tour), *Tiny Plays for Ireland 1 and 2* by 50 writers (Project Arts Centre, Dublin), *The Great Goat Bubble* by Julian Gough (Galway Arts Festival), *The Wheelchair on My Face* by Sonya Kelly (Irish tour and to Paris, Edinburgh and New York), *The End of the Road* by Gavin Kostick (offsite in Temple Bar, Dublin), multi-award winning *Silent* by Pat Kinevane (Irish tour and Europe, Australia and US), *Forgotten* by Pat Kinevane (throughout Ireland and Europe and US), the multi award-winning *The Pride of Parnell Street* by Sebastian Barry (Irish tour, London, New Haven–US, Paris and Wiesbaden), a reading of *My Name Is Rachel Corrie* (Dublin) in association with *Amnesty International* and co-produced and stage-directed *Rank* by Robert Massey (Dublin Theatre Festival and London). Marketa's producing credits for The Performance Corporation include *Slattery's Sago Saga* by Arthur Riordan, *Power Point* by Tom Swift, Theatrical Espressos *KISS USA* and *GAA!* and the Irish premiere of the multi-disciplinary piece *Cool Fresh Milk*. In 2010, Marketa also produced *The Performance Corporation's* SPACE Production Award in association with Absolut Fringe: *From the Heart* by Louise White and Kate Nic Chonaonaigh, *True Enough!* by Making Strange and *Help Me! Help Me!* by Priscilla Robinson.

SABINE DARGENT (Set Designer)
Sabine always enjoys working with Jim Culleton and Fishamble: The New Play Company and has previously designed set and costumes for numerous Fishamble productions including *Tiny Plays For Ireland 1* and *2*, *The Great Goat Bubble*, *Strandline*, *The Pride of Parnell Street*, *Monged*, *Pilgrims in the Park* and *Tadhg Stray Wandered In*. She is the winner of two Irish Times Best Set Design Awards and has been nominated for two others. She works frequently with director Mikel Murfi and designed the set and costumes for *The Walworth Farce* (Druid/world tour). She won the Irish Times Best Set Design Theatre Award in 2006 with her set design for *Hysteria* for B*spoke. Other work includes *It Does Only Happen in Movies*, *Arragh na Pogue*, *B for Baby*, *Penelope* (Druid/world tour; *The Lonesome West* (Lyric, Belfast); and with Enda Walsh on *The New Electric Ballroom* (Druid/world tour); set design with director Conall Morrison includes *Sive*, *The Bacchae of Baghdad*, *The Importance of Being Earnest* (all at the Abbey); *The Crucible* (Lyric, Belfast); *Re-Energize*, *Antigone*, *Hard to Believe* and *Ghosts* which won The Irish Times, Best Set Design Award in 2003. She has also designed sets for Michael Keegan Dolan and Fabulous Beast Dance Theatre for *Helen and Hell*, *Rian* (Bessie Awards). She has worked with numerous other directors and companies and has designed street-theatre costumes, props and floats for the St Patrick Festival: *City Fusion* and *Brighter Future* over the last 7 years.

KEVIN SMITH (Lighting Designer)
Kevin trained at the Samuel Beckett Centre, Trinity College Dublin. He previously designed *These Halcyon Days* by Deirdre Kinahan, which premiered at Dublin Theatre Festival 2012 and went on to play a national tour and in Edinburgh Festival Fringe, where it won a Fringe First Award. It subsequently transferred to New York. Other theatre design credits include: *Romeo and Juliet* (Second Age); *Serious Money*, *Dying City* (Rough Magic); *Grumpy Old Women* (Gaiety); *Rhinoceros* (Blue Raincoat); *Scenes from the Big Picture* (The Lir) and *Beowulf: The Blockbuster* (Pat Moylan Productions). Most recently Kevin designed *Moll* (Verdant/Gaiety Production). Kevin's dance design credits include: *Exodus*, *Grand Junction* (Dance Theatre of Ireland); *The Ballet Ruse* (Muirne Bloomer and Emma O'Kane); *Step Up* with John Jaspers, Liz Roche, John Scott and Marguerite Donlon, and *An Outside Understanding* with Croí Glan (nominated for Best Design in Absolute Fringe 2012). Opera work includes: *Madama Butterfly* (Opera Ireland); *Motion of the Heart* (eX Music Ensemble) and *Flatpack* (Ulysses Opera, nominated for Best Opera Production in last year's Irish Times Theatre Awards). Most recently Kevin designed *Opera Briefs* with The Lir.

LÉONORE MCDONAGH (Costume Designer)

Léonore previously designed costumes for Fishamble: The New Play Company's *Strandline, Handel's Crossing, Pilgrims in the Park, The Buddhist of Castleknock, Moonlight and Music, The Great Jubilee, Doom Raider, The Flesh Addict* and *Jack Ketch's Gallows Jig*. Léonore is an award-winning, freelance costume designer. She studied Fashion Design at Limerick School of Art and Design and has a Masters in History of Art and Design from the National College of Art and Design, Dublin. She has designed costumes for over a hundred shows including theatre, dance, opera, pantomime and street theatre here in Ireland and in the West End, and Europe. In Ireland she has designed for many theatre companies including the Gate Theatre, the Abbey Theatre, the Gaiety, the Olympia, Project Arts Centre, Tivoli Theatre, Second Age Theatre Company, Storytellers Theatre Company, Team Theatre Company, Red Kettle Theatre Company, the Everyman Palace, Cork Opera House, Siamsa Tíre, Galway Youth Theatre, Gallowglass Theatre Company and Island Theatre Company.

DENIS CLOHESSY (Sound Designer/Composer)

Denis has designed sound for Fishamble: The New Play Company's *Strandline, The Pride of Parnell Street* and *Silent*. He has produced work for theatre and dance with the Abbey Theatre, Gate Theatre, Rough Magic, The Corn Exchange, Junk Ensemble and many others. He won the Irish Times Irish Theatre Award for Best Design Sound in 2011, was an associate artist with the Abbey in 2008 and was a participant on Rough Magic's ADVANCE programme in 2012. He has also composed extensively for film and television including *The Land of the Enlightened* (Fastnet Films); *The Irish Pub* (Atom Films); *His and Hers* (Venom Film); *The Reluctant Revolutionary* (Underground Films) and the television series *Limits of Liberty* (South Wind Blows) performed by the RTÉ Concert Orchestra.

GAVIN KOSTICK (Dramaturg)

As Literary Officer at Fishamble: The New Play Company, Gavin works with new writers for theatre through script development for production, readings and a variety of mentorship programmes. Gavin is also an award-winning playwright. He has written over twenty plays, which have been produced nationally and internationally. Recent works include *The End of the Road* for Fishamble; *This is What We Sang* for Kabosh (Belfast and New York); *The Sit* and *Fight Night* on tour 2011 and *An Image for the Rose* outdoors for Whiplash Theatre Company. His latest work *The Games People Play* for RISE Productions has won the Irish Times Irish Theatre Award for Best New Play 2013. He wrote the libretto for *The Alma Fetish*, composed by Raymond Deane, which was staged in 2013 by Wide Open Opera at the National Concert Hall. As a performer, he performed Joseph Conrad's *Heart of Darkness: Complete*, a six-hour show for Absolut Fringe, Dublin Theatre Festival and the London Festival of Literature at the Southbank.

Fishamble Needs Your Support

Become a Friend of Fishamble today and support new theatre making at its best, whilst enjoying the benefits of complimentary tickets, discounts on playwriting courses and exclusive Friends events.

For further information see **www.fishamble.com/support-us** or contact Marketa Dowling on **01 6704018.**

Director's Note

At Fishamble, we commission, develop and produce new plays and have a range of initiatives to support others who are also dedicated to new work. We are always seeking ways to present the best new plays possible and to engage with our audiences in Dublin, throughout Ireland and, increasingly, internationally. In 2011, with this mission in mind, we invited people to send us a tiny play about contemporary life in Ireland, and received over 1,700 submissions. We staged 50 of them in two productions, *Tiny Plays for Ireland 1 & 2*, during 2012 and 2013. Two of the tiny plays we staged were subsequently developed into full-length works: a tiny play by Colin Murphy about the moment the Irish government decided to guarantee the banks became *Guaranteed!* which Fishamble toured extensively last year; and a tiny play *Broken* by Deirdre Kinahan has been developed to become *Spinning*.

Broken was complete in itself, a beautifully judged tiny play set at the school gates, about a father who is prevented from collecting his daughter by the Principal. Deirdre and ourselves then discussed the possibility of a larger play about a separated father, who has lost access to his child, whose life spins out of control, and who turns to desperate measures. We commissioned Deirdre to write *Spinning*, exploring broken characters' search for forgiveness and hope, in the aftermath of a tragic incident. Deirdre is very curious about human nature and brave in the way she tackles issues that are challenging and provocative head-on. Her writing is full of humanity and empathy for her characters, as we saw in her recent plays, including *Bogboy, Moment* and *These Halcyon Days*. *Spinning* also has these trademark qualities, and a fascinating theatrical form as Deirdre delves into the characters' memories, and time shifts back and forth, just as the sea ebbs and flows in the seaside town where the action is set.

I am delighted to be working on this new play with such a strong design, production and administrative team, and a cast of top actors. Thanks to the Arts Council, Dublin City Council, Culture Ireland and all the Friends of Fishamble who make this work possible.

This is the ninth Fishamble production to premiere in the Dublin Theatre Festival; most recently we have presented Sebastian Barry's *The Pride of Parnell Street*, last year's *The Bruising of Clouds* by Sean P Maguire and an In Development presentation of Pat Kinevane's *Silent*, which has just been performed in Serbia and Cavan, and is about to tour to Monaghan and Finland! We hope that audiences will continue to engage with, and enjoy, Fishamble's work through this production of Deirdre Kinahan's *Spinning*.

Jim Culleton

Author's Note

The idea for *Spinning* grew initially from a report on a tragic case of parental abduction circa 2003, and never really faded. It spun around in my head for years as I began to wonder about what happens when love turns – what happens when the power of an intense familiar emotion turns from positive to dangerous.

When Fishamble advertised for Tiny Plays in 2012, plays that reflected issues and concerns of contemporary Ireland, I returned to the idea and thought to write a tiny fragment… a beginning.

I believe that there has been a quiet revolution here in Ireland with the advent of separation and divorce. And while most families cope terrifically, indeed benefit by this new reality, there are others who get lost within it, broken by it. I wanted to try to understand that.

Spinning became a psychological drama charting the journey of two central characters as they attempt to piece together, to process a cathartic and deeply tragic incident in their lives. The audience, like the characters, become detectives, sifting through memory and sifting through story to try to get to the emotional and factual truth.

Spinning is as much an exploration of identity as it is the questioning of a distressing contemporary phenomenon. Marriage and family is so much a part of a person's fabric, that when it breaks down it can tear away at who you believe yourself to be. In this play Conor cannot cope with the failure of his marriage. He loses all perspective and sees the world only in terms of grief and betrayal. He mourns his wife, his daughter, his home, his electric gates and his status. Conor no longer knows who he can be.

Susan, on the other hand, is a lone parent devoting her life to her daughter Annie. It is a good life and they have a warm and loving relationship, but in the aftermath of tragedy everything she thought she had achieved as a mother is questioned. Her sense of self is deeply compromised.

And so we meet these characters. We meet them as they face each other. Face their past and try to understand it. Their journey becomes our journey because if they can find forgiveness, if they can find redemption, empathy… perhaps so can we.

Deirdre Kinahan

Deirdre would like to thank Curtis Brown, Gersh, The Meath County Council Arts Office, Solstice Arts Centre, The Irish Theatre Institute, Project AC, Anne Clarke, Culture Ireland, Maureen Collender, Nick Hern, Tilestyle, The Bailey Family, The Stewart Parker Trust and the Kinahan/O'Farrell family for their constant support of her writing and Fishamble and Mary Banotti in particular for their support on *Spinning*.

SPINNING

Deirdre Kinahan

.

Characters

CONOR, *forty-two in present day*
SUSAN, *forty-four in present day*
ANNIE, *sixteen always*
JEN, *thirty-nine in present day*

The present day for this play is 2014.

The incident at the pier took place in February 2010.

Author's Note

I see a very fluid impressionistic set. The actors walk through to
scenes as we leap through timeline and story. Projections and
the occasional prop and a strong soundscape create the world.
The world is shifting, unreliable, it is defined by memory. The
developing connection between Conor and Susan is the present:
it is the spine of the play, the present reality. The past
encroaches on it. Surrounds it. The past insists on being played.
It spins constantly through the consciousness of these two
characters in their quest for peace and/or understanding.

D.K.

*This text went to press before the end of rehearsals and so may
differ slightly from the play as performed.*

Present day.

CONOR *stands downstage. It is early morning and he is on a small pier in a seaside village. He is looking into the sea. Beat.*

Lights come up on a floor-to-ceiling café window with door attached. It is standalone and upstage of the audience with a table and two chairs standing in front... In the world of the play it faces the pier. A woman, SUSAN, stands in the window looking out at CONOR.

CONOR *turns to see her standing there. Beat.*

SUSAN *opens the door setting off a small bell. She stands outside the café.*

SUSAN   I know who you are.

CONOR   I know.

          Pause.

SUSAN   You have no right...

          You have no right to be here.

CONOR   I'm sorry.

SUSAN   You're what?

CONOR   I don't know what else to do.

SUSAN   You don't know what else to do?

CONOR   No.

SUSAN   But haven't you done enough?

          Haven't you done enough to me?

          Pause.

CONOR   I would like...

          I wonder if...

          I wonder if I could talk to you...

SUSAN   Jesus…

          Jesus Christ!

CONOR   Because maybe I can explain…

SUSAN   Explain?

CONOR   Or try to… try to explain, Susan…

SUSAN   Don't say my name.

          Don't you ever.

          Ever.

          Dirty me… or say my name.

CONOR   I'm sorry.

SUSAN   I want you to stop.

          To stop… being here.

CONOR   Okay.

          But he doesn't move.

          But I don't know where else to go.

SUSAN   This will kill me.

          Don't you see that.

          This will kill me too.

CONOR   I don't want… I never wanted to hurt anyone.

          She gasps.

          I just… I just want to talk… please.

          Just talk… because I wish… I wish…

SUSAN   And do you want to know what I wish?

          Do you want to know what I wish, Conor Bourke?

CONOR   No.

          I mean yes.

          Yes of course, I do want to know.

SUSAN   I wish it was you that drowned that day. I wish it
          was YOU. And that the rocks had made ribbons of
          you. And that your stinking corpse was left rotting
          there... just pickings for the gulls.

CONOR   Okay.

          Pause.

          I understand.

SUSAN   No you don't understand.

          If you did... you wouldn't be here.

CONOR   But I think the same.

          I wish the same sometimes.

          Pause.

SUSAN   I'd kill you myself you know.

          Right now.

          If I had the means.

          Pause.

CONOR   Okay.

SUSAN   Okay?

CONOR   Yes. That's okay.

          You have the means.

          He indicates the sea.

          Just push me over.

          She turns her back to him in disgust.

SUSAN   Christ.

          She makes to return to the café.

CONOR   I mean it.

          I think I'm finished.

SUSAN   And do you expect me to care?

          Do you dare...

CONOR   No.

          No.

          I don't expect anyone to care.

          It's just… I have something for you.

SUSAN   You what?

CONOR   I have something for you.

          She stalls.

SUSAN   Please tell me how this is happening?

          Who lets this happen?

          Who lets you be here… at my café.

CONOR   It's over now…

SUSAN   Over!… Over?

          How can it ever be over for me?!

          He takes a chain from his pocket.

CONOR   I have Annie's locket.

          She is shocked.

          It's yours. It should always have been yours.

          He holds it out in his hand.

          I want to return it.

          She doesn't move. She doesn't respond.

          I know it was important.

          A birthday present.

SUSAN   Stop.

CONOR   She loved it.

SUSAN   Stop!

CONOR   And I've had it all this time.

SUSAN   How…?

CONOR   It was in my pocket. And I thought about posting it... after... later... when I was... But that didn't seem right somehow.

Do you want it?

SUSAN   Oh God.

She almost collapses into the chair.

He puts it onto the table in front of her.

CONOR   Annie would want you to have it.

SUSAN   (*Sharp*.) How do you know?!

How do you know that, you bastard?

How do you know what Annie might want?!

The lighting changes. There is the projection of a Ferris wheel. We shift now to the past. It is a funfair four years earlier and ANNIE is standing under the Ferris wheel. CONOR leaves SUSAN (who remains at the table and on stage) and enters the scene.

He is walking past ANNIE in the past with two boxes of chips.

ANNIE   Give us one, why don't you!

CONOR   What?

ANNIE   Give us one of your chips.

CONOR   Oh, sure!

She takes one.

Careful, they're hot!

ANNIE   I know.

CONOR   Right.

ANNIE   Who's the other one for?

CONOR   What?

ANNIE   The other carton.

CONOR   ...no one.

ANNIE   I see.

CONOR   Okay...

          He is about to leave.

ANNIE   Have you just got in then?

CONOR   Got in?

ANNIE   To town.

CONOR   Oh yeah.

ANNIE   For the mid-term is it?

CONOR   Yeah.

          She takes another chip.

ANNIE   And you're from Dublin?

CONOR   No.

ANNIE   Where?

CONOR   Full of questions, aren't you?!

ANNIE   Yeah.

          She grins.

          And chips!

          She takes another chip. He smiles.

CONOR   You can have them...

ANNIE   No thanks.

          My friend will just scoff them.

CONOR   Who's your friend?

ANNIE	She's up there.
	She points to the Ferris wheel.
	Claire.
	She loves the wheel.
CONOR	And you don't?
ANNIE	No.
	It's boring.
	Same rides every year.
CONOR	Right.
	Slight pause.
ANNIE	So where are you staying?
CONOR	Where am I staying?
ANNIE	The cottages?
CONOR	No.
ANNIE	Just as well. They're poxy, the cottages. My mam says they built them on the Marsh during the boom, so they're always flooding... they stink.
CONOR	Do they?
ANNIE	Yeah.
CONOR	Well I'm not staying in the cottages.
ANNIE	Good.
	Slight pause.
CONOR	I think your wheel is slowing down.
ANNIE	So it is.
	He starts to leave.
CONOR	Say hi to Claire.
ANNIE	Why don't you come meet her for yourself?
CONOR	Because I've got to get back.

ANNIE   To no one?

         He smiles.

         Why don't you meet us later?

CONOR   What?

ANNIE   In the pub.

CONOR   You're joking!

ANNIE   Why would I be joking?

CONOR   Because I'm too old.

ANNIE   You're not so old.

CONOR   Too old for you!

ANNIE   I'm seventeen!

CONOR   Jesus.

ANNIE   What's wrong with that?

CONOR   Just go and find your pal!

ANNIE   I will so!

         He walks away, she shouts after him.

         We're here most nights all the same… if you can
         get away from 'no one'?!

         At this point JEN *comes on stage to set up the next
         scene.*

CONOR   I'll keep that in mind.

ANNIE   …Annie!

CONOR   Annie.

         He smiles. She smiles and watches him go.

The lighting changes. CONOR *takes off his coat and walks into the next scene to* JEN, *his ex-wife. We are further in the past now. Twelve years previous to the present day. We are in a nightclub. The music is beating loudly.* CONOR *is in a corner with* JEN. *They are obviously keeping a lid on their relationship. Their conversation is taut with desire…*

CONOR   You are so fucking beautiful.

JEN   Well I dressed just for you.

CONOR   Fuck.

       You drive me nuts… you know that?

JEN   I know.

CONOR   Are you going to tell him?

JEN   Yes.

CONOR   When?

JEN   Tonight, I told you, tonight.

CONOR   So tell him!

JEN   Not here.

       When we go home.

CONOR   Home?

       I can't wait that long.

JEN   You can.

CONOR   I want you right now.

       I want it right now, Jen.

JEN   I know.

       So do I.

CONOR   But I want the whole lot.

JEN   I know.

CONOR   No messin' now. The house. The couch.

          The life... your life... I want it all.

JEN   Is this a proposal?

CONOR   You know what I'm saying!

JEN   It's some proposal!

CONOR   (*Sharp.*) Don't laugh at me.

JEN   I'm not laughing at you, Conor.

          Just slow down.

CONOR   I can't. I love you. I so fucking love you. And I'm home now. I'm back. I'm not letting anyone else. It's too important. This is too important, isn't it, Jen? You're the same. You've got to tell me you feel the same?

JEN   I do.

CONOR   So I don't want you going home with him.

JEN   I have to be fair, Conor.

          It's been two years...

CONOR   But no kissing... no touching... I couldn't stand it.

JEN   You're the one who went away...

CONOR   That was a mistake.

JEN   Okay but you've got to let me do this properly.

CONOR   I thought of you every day, Jen. I swear. You're the reason I came back. I could have had any one of those Aussie birds but it's not the same... they don't smell the same.

          She laughs again.

          Why the fuck are you laughing?

          His response is a little strong but she brushes it off.

JEN   Well what exactly do I smell like?

CONOR   Grass... yeah, grass... and beautiful sex.

          He nuzzles into her.

JEN   Stop. Please. I really don't want Ryan to see us.

CONOR   Poor bastard's going to hate losing you.

          She looks across the nightclub.

JEN   I dunno... he has his rugby.

CONOR   He's crazy.

JEN   Maybe it's me who's crazy...

CONOR   Come outside with me now.

JEN   No.

CONOR   They won't see.

JEN   I'm afraid they already see.

CONOR   Come on, Jen.

          *She pulls her face away but takes his hand
          decisively and they leave.*

          SUSAN *picks up the locket, the lighting changes
          and we return to the present.*

CONOR   I want you to know that I wasn't always like
          this... like that.

SUSAN   Why?

CONOR   Why what?

SUSAN   Why do you want me to know?

CONOR   Because... I never meant... I never intended...

SUSAN   Oh please...

CONOR   I was out of control.

          It all just got out of control.

SUSAN   Yes.

          That's what you said in court.

          And it worked so well... it worked so well for you
          didn't it, Conor Bourke, Oak Road, Athboy,
          County Meath.

          Your Depression.

          Your Crisis.

          YOUR horseshit.

CONOR   It wasn't horseshit.

SUSAN   (*Angrily.*) It won you that sentence!

          He doesn't respond.

          Four years... FOUR YEARS.

          For MY daughter and MY life.

CONOR   Maybe it wasn't enough...

SUSAN   It was all we were worth to the world.

          Pause.

CONOR   I know how much she loved you.

SUSAN   (*With sarcasm.*) Do you?

CONOR   And I know your grief.

SUSAN   (*Incredulous.*) Ha!

CONOR   I don't see Jen either.

          And I don't see Kate.

SUSAN   That's hardly surprising.

CONOR   No.

          Pause.

SUSAN   You don't know my grief!

          Every day. EV-ERY day I ask the same question. I
          ask the pillow. I ask the floor. The toaster. The

toothbrush. The gulls. I even ask that fucker God in his heaven... why Annie? Why my Annie?

But I never dreamt. I never dreamt... that the only... the only man who could tell me... would show up at my door.

CONOR   I don't know why.

I don't know why Annie...

SUSAN   Don't say that.

CONOR   I'm sorry...

She almost growls.

SUSAN   Why her?

ANNIE walks on stage now and takes the locket gently from SUSAN then puts it around her neck. She walks SUSAN into the next scene. CONOR remains upstage at the window, watching.

It is the past and we are in ANNIE and SUSAN's home... ANNIE is curling SUSAN's hair with tongs.

ANNIE   Hold still, Mam.

SUSAN   If you make an arse of this, Annie, I'll kill you.

ANNIE   I won't.

SUSAN   And I won't have time to wash it again.

ANNIE   Just relax!

Have your glass of wine and pretend you're in the salon.

SUSAN   When am I ever in the salon?!

ANNIE   Just PRETEND, okay!

SUSAN	Okay.
	And, Annie?
ANNIE	Yeah?
SUSAN	Would I smell burning in 'the salon'?
ANNIE	Shit!
SUSAN	For God's sake…
ANNIE	It's just a singe.
	And look! A lovely curl.

SUSAN *looks in the mirror.*

SUSAN	Not bad.
ANNIE	Can I do the rest?
SUSAN	Go on so.

ANNIE *starts another curl.*

ANNIE	Can I have a glass of wine?
SUSAN	No.
ANNIE	Why not?
SUSAN	You're not eighteen.
ANNIE	You know I have the odd glass.
SUSAN	You'll have my hair in flames!
ANNIE	Hardly, Mam… I'll be fine!
SUSAN	Go on so.

ANNIE *gets a glass and pours, delighted.*

ANNIE	I'll do your toes too if you like.
SUSAN	With the tongs!

They both laugh.

ANNIE	Are you wearing sandals?
SUSAN	No.

ANNIE   What shoes are you wearing?

SUSAN   I don't know. You can help me choose when I put
           on the dress.

ANNIE   You're looking good, Mam.

SUSAN   Am I?

ANNIE   YES!

           Is there going to be music?

SUSAN   Of course.

           It's a party.

           Are you sure you don't want to come?

ANNIE   Sure.

           Claire's coming over…

SUSAN   But can't Claire come too?

           You're on your holidays…

ANNIE   No, it's not our scene…

SUSAN   I don't like leaving you…

ANNIE   I'm not a child, Mam, for God's sake, I babysit
           children myself! Now you need to wear a pair of
           shoes you can dance in.

SUSAN   But you love a do in the hotel?!

ANNIE   It'll be all auld ones!

SUSAN   Oh… thank you very much.

ANNIE   You know what I mean.

SUSAN   I suppose I do.

           Pause as she does her hair.

ANNIE   Will you have a fortieth?

SUSAN   No.

ANNIE   Why not?

SUSAN	What's to celebrate?
ANNIE	It's a birthday, Mam.
SUSAN	I'd rather you and me went away.
ANNIE	Really?
SUSAN	Yeah.
ANNIE	Is that what you're thinking?
SUSAN	I suppose. I don't know. I haven't made any plans.
ANNIE	I'd love that, Mam.
SUSAN	Would you?
ANNIE	Yeah.
	To a nice hotel.
SUSAN	Why not?
ANNIE	We haven't gone away in ages.
SUSAN	I know.
	I'm sorry.
ANNIE	Don't be sorry.
	This is great.
	We'll pick somewhere posh... in Dublin... or Galway?
SUSAN	Sure.
	I don't mind.
ANNIE	This is deadly!
SUSAN	And are you sure you want to come away with this auld one?
ANNIE	Mam!
	Are you mad.
	We'll have a blast!
SUSAN	Great. That's settled then.
	We'll have a look on the internet.

ANNIE   I can do it tonight when you're out.

           The tongs hit SUSAN*'s head.*

SUSAN   Jesus! Mind my head!

ANNIE   Sorry!

           She kisses the spot where she burnt it.

           I'll top up your wine.

SUSAN   Good girl!

ANNIE   I love you, Mam.

SUSAN   I love you too.

           JEN *comes on stage and takes the glass of wine
           out of* SUSAN*'s hand and lies on a couch. The
           lighting changes. It is the past.* JEN *is hugely
           pregnant. We are in* CONOR *and* JEN*'s sitting
           room.* CONOR *enters.*

CONOR   You're drinking wine?

           She is surprised to see him.

JEN   Just a small glass.

CONOR   At this hour?

JEN   The book says it might help me relax…

CONOR   I don't think that's wise, Jen.

           He takes it from her.

JEN   Okay!… It's half lemonade anyway.

           What are you doing home?

CONOR   Mammy rang me. She said you were here. That
           you had to leave work…?

JEN	I felt hot.
CONOR	You see you shouldn't be still at work at this stage, Jen.
JEN	I finish at the end of the week.
CONOR	But Mammy says you shouldn't go back.
JEN	Your mammy isn't having this baby, Conor.
	For Christ's sake.
CONOR	She just worries.
JEN	I'm fine.
CONOR	And I worry!
JEN	I'm fine!
CONOR	I brought you doughnuts.
JEN	Oh... thanks.
CONOR	Are you sure you're fine?
JEN	Yes I'm sure.
	What are you like!?

He comes around and lifts her legs so he can sit under them. She pulls his hand onto her belly.

CONOR	I'm off work myself for the day now!
JEN	So who's minding the shop?
CONOR	Mammy.
JEN	She's supposed to have retired?
CONOR	She set it up, Jen...
JEN	Like I haven't heard that before!
CONOR	She built it up to 'what it is today'–
JEN	(*In tandem.*) 'What it is today'! I know.
CONOR	She just loves it...
JEN	I know, Conor, and that's why you'll never be rid of her.

CONOR   Anyway she's convinced you'll 'go' today?

JEN   She's convinced I'll 'go' every day.

CONOR   Ger McGoona told her you'd 'go' today.

JEN   Ger McGoona?

         Is that the bloody fortune-teller?

CONOR   With a direct line to your uterus apparently!

JEN   I'm not sure I can take this any more.

CONOR   Relax. She's just excited.

         First grandchild!

JEN   She's just a fucking pressure is what she is!

         She's on the phone on the hour!

         (*Imitating* CONOR*'s mother.*) 'Do you think you might "go"!'

CONOR   You're brilliant, Jen.

JEN   I'm not brilliant.

         I can't make it start.

         I can't make it 'go'.

CONOR   Will I make you a cup of tea so?

JEN   No!

CONOR   You've done everything right, Jen.

         You'll be grand.

JEN   Will I?

CONOR   Give us a kiss…

JEN   You'll have to climb the mountain first!

CONOR   It's beautiful.

         And I bet she's beautiful.

         I can't wait to see her.

He kisses her pregnant belly.

JEN   How do you know it's a her?

CONOR   I just do.

             Only a girl can come from you.

JEN   I don't think that's technically true!

CONOR   I know!

             He speaks to the belly.

             But we know, don't we, gorgeous!

             You're gonna be Daddy's girl.

             The belly moves.

             Did you see that?

             She knows me. She knows my voice.

JEN   Of course she does.

             Slight pause.

             I'm glad you're home now.

CONOR   Yeah, it's great isn't it!

JEN   And you don't have to go back?

CONOR   No!

JEN   Come on up here so.

             She shifts over on the couch.

CONOR   What?

JEN   Come on…

CONOR   But are you sure it's all right to have sex?

JEN   Yes.

             The book actually says it's good for me.

CONOR   It does?

JEN   Might even help me 'go'…!

CONOR   I dunno, Jen... maybe I should ask my mammy!

*She laughs and throws a cushion at him as he
wriggles up the couch to kiss her. They kiss.*

*SUSAN lights up a cigarette. This pulls CONOR
back to the present. The lighting changes.
CONOR and SUSAN are still sitting at the table
outside the café.*

SUSAN   Did you love her?

CONOR   What?

SUSAN   Did you love Annie?

CONOR   I loved... I love Jen...

She pulls on her cigarette.

SUSAN   Then were you lovers?

Did you make Annie your lover?

I'd like to know because that's the only way it
makes sense to me. That's the only way it makes
sense to me that she was there...

CONOR   ...no...

SUSAN   And I want the truth.

No more of your bullshit.

CONOR   We weren't lovers.

She examines him.

I was clear about that.

The coroner...

Pause.

It was always clear.

SUSAN   I don't believe you.

CONOR   Not in the sense, Susan... not in the sense that you're saying...

SUSAN   What sense then?

CONOR   We just weren't... lovers.

She is silent for a beat.

SUSAN   Well. Do you want to hear something tragic? Do you want to hear something tragic, Conor Bourke?... I think I'm disappointed. Yes, I am. I'm disappointed because a part of me would like that... A part of me would like to know that Annie knew love... at the end.

Because she was so young. And so ready... so ready to take on her life, her place in the world. She was beautiful. So beautiful. And even if it was you. Even if it was a despicable bastard like you. IF she wanted you... I'd like her to have known 'love'.

She sucks hard on her cigarette.

CONOR   She was just a kid.

Just a child in my eyes.

SUSAN   MY child.

CONOR   Yes. Your child...

ANNIE *enters. The lighting changes. It is the past.*
CONOR *goes over to a bench and sits. We are in*
a playground. ANNIE *sees him and hops up onto*
the back of the bench.

ANNIE   Hello!

CONOR   Oh hello.

ANNIE   How's the holiday going?

CONOR   The holiday?

          Oh it's great... yes, it's going great.

ANNIE   I haven't seen you round?

CONOR   Well I've been around.

ANNIE   Really?

CONOR   Yeah.

ANNIE   Okay.

          But what are you doing here?

CONOR   Here?

ANNIE   At the playground.

CONOR   I'm watching my daughter.

ANNIE   Oh!

CONOR   Is that all right?

ANNIE   That's just fine.

CONOR   Good.

ANNIE   I knew you couldn't be on your own.

CONOR   Why?

ANNIE   Just did.

          Pause.

          So which one is yours?

CONOR   She's on the pirate boat...

ANNIE	With the pink shoes?
CONOR	Yes.
ANNIE	She's cute.
CONOR	She is.
ANNIE	How old?
CONOR	She's six.

He waves to the girl in the playground.

And she loves that boat!

Pause.

ANNIE	You don't wear a wedding ring?
CONOR	No.
ANNIE	So you're not married?

He looks at her exasperated.

CONOR	I'm not any more.

She laughs.

And what are you doing here?

ANNIE	I'm waiting for Claire.
CONOR	Again!
ANNIE	This is where we hang.
CONOR	Is it?
ANNIE	Yes.

I'm just a bit early.

She takes out a cigarette and lights it.

Do you want one?

CONOR	No.

You shouldn't be smoking.

ANNIE	I know.

CONOR   So why do you?

ANNIE   Because it looks cool.

CONOR   That's daft.

ANNIE   I know that too.

She blows smoke into the air...

What's your name?

CONOR   ...Conor.

ANNIE   I like that.

CONOR   You're something else!

Do you know that, Annie!

ANNIE   Oh! You remember!

CONOR   Of course I remember.

ANNIE   I made an impression so!

CONOR   You did.

Slight pause.

ANNIE   So is it just the two of you then on holiday?

CONOR   It is.

ANNIE   My mam's on her own.

It never bothered me.

CONOR   Good.

ANNIE   I can babysit if you like?

If you want a pint?

CONOR   No thanks.

ANNIE   I'm only eight euro an hour.

That's minimum wage.

CONOR   I'm alright.

Slight pause.

ANNIE	I used to wish I had a sister.
CONOR	So does Kate.
ANNIE	Well there you go then!
	We could be company.

CONOR gets up to go.

CONOR	I better go… she looks like she's getting tired.
ANNIE	I'm always here… or up at the fair… if you change your mind.
CONOR	Okay. Thanks.

This scene is interrupted now by JEN and another memory.

JEN	Did you change your mind?
ANNIE	Byee.

He smiles.

CONOR	Bye.

CONOR now enters into the next scene. To JEN.

The lighting changes. We are in the past, in CONOR and JEN's house. JEN is on her laptop on the couch… CONOR has just put their daughter to bed.

JEN	Did you change your mind and read it to her?
CONOR	Yeah.
JEN	I knew it. You have no willpower.
	Just turn off the light and close the door.
CONOR	She likes it when I read to her.
JEN	How many times?

CONOR	What?
JEN	How many times did you read that story?

He laughs.

CONOR	Four!
JEN	Jesus... you spoil her, Conor!
CONOR	She's spoilable...
JEN	She needs to learn to get to sleep on her own.
CONOR	Would you listen to Super Nanny!
JEN	(*Good-humouredly.*) Piss off.

He flops down beside her.

CONOR	You even look the part; in your slippers and your specs.
JEN	This is my studious look.

He starts to kiss her neck.

CONOR	It does it for me.
JEN	Go away, I'm trying to read these plans.
CONOR	What plans?
JEN	They're for the new apartments.

I told you, Ryan asked me to handle the sales.

CONOR	Ryan?

He pauses.

Are you serious about this?

JEN	You know I am.
CONOR	But we haven't really discussed it.
JEN	We have. I told you it's just a few hours a week. Mostly evenings and weekends.
CONOR	And 'I told you' you don't need to go back to work.

The shop is booming.

JEN   This has nothing to do with the shop.

               This is for me.

CONOR   Weekends?

JEN   Occasionally.

CONOR   But we love our weekends?

               We love Sunday at Mammy's!...

JEN   No. You love Sunday at Mammy's.

CONOR   But we'll miss you...

JEN   No you won't.

               I'll be just round the corner!

               She gives him a kiss. Then hops up.

               I got us some nice steaks.

               She disappears.

CONOR   I'll cook them.

               He doesn't move.

JEN   (*Off.*) Of course. I'll do the salad.

               He broods. Beat.

               The memory above is interrupted now by SUSAN
               in the present.

SUSAN   I thought I knew her.

               The lighting changes accordingly and CONOR
               returns to the conversation with SUSAN *in the
               present.*

               I thought I knew every hair of her... every
               thought... and every trick...

CONOR   She loved you.

               She stares at him with such loathing... he is silent.

SUSAN   It was like we were connected.

From the first.

And we were, of course we were...

Because she came from me.

I remember when she was a baby I would wake just as she stirred for milk... and I would feel her hunger in my breast... and my eyes would always open just before hers... it's animal, it's primal... that connection. And as she grew up... she could take the thought right out of my head... just lift it right out... like the day, that day she said 'I don't want me to go to school either, Mammy... why don't I stay with you here, in the café'...

She smiles.

She knew that's just what I was thinking. She heard me think it, she heard me even though I never said a word.

Because she was... she was all I had in the world.

And I never expected that.

I never expected to be... alone.

CONOR   No.

Pause.

SUSAN   But I never knew about you!

Now, how is that? I never checked. I never heard...

And not even Claire...

When I went through it all with Claire... after... afterward. When I asked her and I asked her... about you... about that week... she said... she SWORE...

She didn't know.... None of us... None of us knew about you.

CONOR   No.

SUSAN   How did I let that happen?

> ANNIE *comes on stage and sits at a kitchen table.*
> *The lighting changes and* SUSAN *joins her.*
> CONOR *remains, watching.*

SUSAN   What time did you get in at?

ANNIE   What?

SUSAN   You heard me, Annie!

ANNIE   I was in all night!

SUSAN   I checked your room at 2 a.m. and there was no sign of you!

ANNIE   I came down here to get a glass of milk.

SUSAN   Will you for God's sake stop lying to me.

          Where were you?

ANNIE   I wasn't anywhere.

SUSAN   What's that on your neck?

ANNIE   Nothing.

SUSAN   It's a hickey.

ANNIE   It's not.

SUSAN   It's a great big dirty hickey... you were out with some boy!

ANNIE   I wasn't.

SUSAN   Which boy?

ANNIE   Please, Mam.

SUSAN   Was it Jason?

ANNIE   No.

SUSAN   I can't stand that Jason.

ANNIE   I know you can't.

          Please leave me alone.

SUSAN   I've warned you about this, Annie.

I've warned you about staying out all night.

You'll get caught!

ANNIE   Caught what?

Caught kissing?

Caught pregnant?

I'm not 'you', Mam. I'm not going to get caught like you. I'm not going to have my life ruined like you. He broke it off. Are you happy? He broke it off because he fancies Claire. So I'm dumped! Not pregnant.

Pause as SUSAN *tries to control her anger.*

SUSAN   You told me you wouldn't see him.

ANNIE   I like him.

SUSAN   He's a thug.

ANNIE   You just think that because of his hair.

SUSAN   I think that because he's a thug.

He's not good enough for you, Annie…

ANNIE   He hates me.

He laughed at me.

So you needn't worry.

SUSAN   Why did he laugh at you?

ANNIE   Because I told him I love him.

SUSAN   Little prick.

Pause.

ANNIE   And I've had the hickey for a week but you're never here so you didn't see it.

SUSAN *sighs.*

SUSAN   I have to work, Annie. You know I have to work.

ANNIE   You don't work evenings!

SUSAN	All I do is pilates!
	For Jesus' sake! I'm entitled to two evenings a week.
	I don't want to get too flabby.
ANNIE	But you're not flabby!
SUSAN	(*Grabbing her love handles.*) I am flabby!
	ANNIE *starts to laugh.*
	Don't laugh.
ANNIE	I can't help it.
	(*Imitating* SUSAN, *grabbing her belly.*) 'I AM flabby!'
	Slight pause.
SUSAN	Getting pregnant didn't ruin my life.
	I've never ever said that.
ANNIE	But you're always alone.
SUSAN	Not always.
ANNIE	I don't want to be alone.
SUSAN	Oh God, Annie… you won't be alone, you're beautiful.
	Pause.
ANNIE	But when do I get to meet Dad?
SUSAN	Dad?
ANNIE	Yes. Dad! I've tried looking him up on Facebook.
	And there were a few Kevin Deans in Melbourne.
SUSAN	But not him?
ANNIE	No.
	Unless he's sixteen.
SUSAN	Benjamin Button!

ANNIE	Why did he never come back?
SUSAN	I've told you, Annie.
ANNIE	You haven't.
SUSAN	He went over without a visa... and neither of us knew about you before he left...
ANNIE	So why didn't you write... or phone... you had phones!
SUSAN	Of course we had phones but we really didn't know each other and I thought we'd be fine... you and me... by ourselves.
ANNIE	So does he even know now?
SUSAN	Of course he does. You know he does.
	But it was too late... by the time... by the time we got in touch...
ANNIE	You should have followed him.
SUSAN	Maybe.
ANNIE	You said he asked?!
SUSAN	He was just being decent, Annie...
	He was... he is decent.
	But it was a long time ago and Granny was too sick.
ANNIE	But Granny's dead now, Mam, and so's Granddad.
	So maybe we could try it?
SUSAN	Try what?
ANNIE	Melbourne!
SUSAN	Melbourne?
ANNIE	I'm sure we could find him!
	And Australia's class, Mam... it's such a class place to live... it's always sunny and there's surf and I watched this programme on canoeing... it

was out in the outback or something... along this river... and I was thinking... maybe he has a ranch...!

SUSAN   For God's sake, Annie. He's probably married now with two kids and a mortgage... he won't want to know about us.

ANNIE   How do you know?

SUSAN   I just know.

ANNIE   Jesus.

SUSAN   What?

ANNIE   You're so dull, Mam.

You're so fucking dull.

SUSAN   Stop... stop before you get into trouble.

ANNIE   But I hate it here. I hate this pissy town and I hate everyone in it. You should have gone after him, Mam... then we could have had a different life.

SUSAN   Our life is not so bad!

ANNIE   Our life is totally crap.

Pause.

SUSAN   You're just upset.

ANNIE   I'm not!

SUSAN   And tired.

ANNIE   I'm not.

SUSAN   That's what you get when you stay out half the night.

ANNIE   I was in Claire's! I was crying in Claire's!

SUSAN   Well that better be the truth, Annie, because I'm ringing her mother...

ANNIE   It is the truth.

SUSAN   You said she went off with Jason!?

ANNIE   She didn't.

          She hates him too.

SUSAN   Oh!

          ...Go, Claire.

ANNIE   Yeah... go, Claire...

SUSAN   Don't do it again. Okay!

          You need to come cry at home.

          I was up all night and now I've to go in and
          open up.

          JEN enters with her laptop. The lighting changes.
          It is the past. We are in JEN *and* CONOR'*s house.*
          JEN *is working at her laptop...* CONOR *leaves*
          his position and enters the scene, car keys in hand.

CONOR   Jen!

JEN   I'm in here.

CONOR   Hiya.

          He gives her a kiss.

JEN   Hi.

CONOR   Where's Kate?

JEN   I'm going to go down and get her now.

CONOR   What?

JEN   Just ten minutes. I need to finish this.

CONOR   You didn't collect her on your way home from
          work?

JEN   I needed to finish this.

CONOR   For Christ's sake, Jen.

          You know I don't like her left late in the crèche...

JEN   The Demense is going on sale tomorrow.

          Ryan needs me to have these contracts.

CONOR   Fuck Ryan.

JEN	Well that's very helpful, Conor, thanks!
CONOR	I can't stand you working there.
JEN	You can't stand me working anywhere.
CONOR	Not this again.
JEN	You started it.
CONOR	You could at least have phoned me.
JEN	I didn't have time!

She's fine.

She's in the crèche.

Please... I don't want a fight.

I just need to finish these contracts.

CONOR	But it's always the same with you...
JEN	It's not...

Slight pause.

Look, why don't you go get her?

You know she loves it when you go get her.

CONOR	For fuck's sake!

I don't know why Mammy can't have her.

JEN	Ughhhh I knew that was next –
CONOR	Because this crèche makes no sense!
JEN	She needs to socialise, Conor.
CONOR	What she needs is a brother or sister!
JEN	Stop! Will you please stop.

We've discussed all this.

And you know your mother would smother her.

CONOR	I know she's a better mother than you, Jen.

She'd never leave my daughter LAST in the crèche...

JEN *is shocked.*

JEN   I just needed ten minutes.

CONOR   So take your ten minutes. I'll go.

               He storms out of the scene and we hear a door slam.

               The lighting changes and CONOR *is back in the present.*

CONOR   I told her not to tell.

               I asked her…

               I needed…

SUSAN   What did you need?

               What the hell did you need?

               You had your own life.

               A Family!

               JEN *now closes the laptop. She pulls her top so it is off the shoulder. It's late. It's the past.* CONOR *and* JEN *have both been out.* CONOR *steps into the scene…*

JEN   Ten grand, Conor Burke!

               CONOR *takes her by the hips and walks/talks her towards the couch.*

CONOR   Yes.

               You're a very clever girl.

JEN   What will we do with it?

CONOR   Anything you like…

He pushes her down onto the couch now and climbs on top.

JEN   And he says I'll get a bonus on the Demense too.

When those houses all go through...

He has pulled off her top and starts kissing her breasts.

CONOR   Clever... clever... girl.

JEN   Let's go on a trip...

He is now kissing her stomach and pulling at her skirt.

CONOR   Okay...

JEN   Let's go to the States or something!

He lifts his head.

CONOR   Are you ever going to stop talking?

She holds his head in her hands.

JEN   The Grand Canyon!

He goes to kiss her... but she pulls back.

Or Mexico!

I've always wanted to go to Mexico!

CONOR   Sure we can just as easy go to Spain.

JEN   Spain?

CONOR   Yeah.

JEN   To your parents' fucking villa?

CONOR   Yeah.

JEN   Is that the height of your ambition, Conor?

The height of your imagination!

CONOR   What are you talking about?

JEN   I want to go on a trip!

An exciting, life-changing trip.

	With my very own ten grand.
	And all you suggest is Spain!
CONOR	What's wrong with Spain?
JEN	We go there every year!
	And with your entire bogger family!
CONOR	So we go on our own?
	Stay longer?
JEN	Jesus.

She wriggles out from underneath him.

| CONOR | What the hell just happened there? |

She stands up. She finds her top.

JEN	What?
CONOR	We were just... weren't we just... hang on, Jen... we were just about to shag!
JEN	That's not the point.
CONOR	The point? Who gives a fuck about the point. I want a shag... I want some sex, Jen... what's going on with you?
JEN	There's nothing going on with me.
CONOR	Come back here...
JEN	No.
CONOR	But what did I do?
JEN	I'm just... not in the mood...
CONOR	You're never in the mood.
JEN	I'm tired.
CONOR	Yet you were fucking firing a minute ago...
JEN	I'm tired of YOU!

Pause.

CONOR   What?

JEN   Nothing.

           He gets up off the couch.

CONOR   What did you say?

JEN   I didn't mean it.

           I don't mean it, I'm sorry.

CONOR   I LOVE you.

           And I WANT you... all the time. But I don't think
           I like this... I don't think I like this change.

JEN   What change?

           Slight pause.

CONOR   When are we having another baby?

           She doesn't answer.

           You agreed, Jen.

           We agreed on another baby!

JEN   Another baby won't solve anything, Conor.

           *She goes to leave. He grabs her arm quite
           violently. She stops, shocked.*

           Let go.

CONOR   No.

JEN   Let go of me.

           He doesn't.

           You can't.

           You can't touch me this way...

           Beat.

           He lets go of her arm.

ANNIE *comes on stage. The lighting changes. It is morning. It is in the past and we are back in the playground.* CONOR *lets go of* JEN. *She exits. He approaches* ANNIE.

CONOR   Hello!

ANNIE   Hi...

CONOR   Fancy seeing you here!

            She shrugs.

            Shouldn't you be at school?

ANNIE   It's just a waste of time.

CONOR   Is it?

ANNIE   Yeah.

CONOR   Haven't you got exams?

ANNIE   Next year... if I stay!

CONOR   Do you plan on going away?

ANNIE   As soon as I can... I'm going to Melbourne.

CONOR   Really?

            I used to live in Sydney.

ANNIE   Fucking A!

CONOR   (*Smiles.*) Maybe.

ANNIE   So why the hell did you come back?

CONOR   I don't know...

            Lots of reasons...

ANNIE   Bet you regret it!

CONOR   Sometimes.

ANNIE   Well when I go... I am never coming back.

CONOR   Won't you get caught up here?... Mitching?

            It's hardly out of sight of the town.

ANNIE	I don't care. I'm shit at school.
	Shit at everything.
CONOR	I can't believe that.
	I'd say you're just having a bad day.
	Pause.
ANNIE	So how come you're still here?
CONOR	What?
ANNIE	The mid-term break is over. All the Dubs are gone.
CONOR	Oh yeah.
ANNIE	Doesn't Kate have to go back to school?
CONOR	Yes, she does.
	Of course she does.
	We're just staying a few extra days.
ANNIE	Why?
CONOR	Em... it's a long story.
	She's up at the house.
ANNIE	On her own?
CONOR	Yeah. But only for a while.
	I'm just on my way to the shop.
ANNIE	So why don't I watch her for you?
CONOR	What?
ANNIE	Don't you need someone to watch her?
CONOR	(*Hesitates.*) I'll only be ten minutes.
ANNIE	But what if she falls?
	What if she's scared? What if...?
CONOR	Okay... okay...
	Maybe I do.

ANNIE   Which house is it?

CONOR   It's… em… sure why don't I bring you up.

SUSAN   Was it some shrink told you to talk to me?

             The lighting changes. CONOR *returns to the present. He doesn't answer.*

             Some shrink from the prison?

CONOR   No.

             Not really.

             She encouraged me to write… to maybe write to you.

SUSAN   Really…?

CONOR   Yeah.

SUSAN   They know nothing.

             Pause.

CONOR   Are you seeing one?

SUSAN   (*Slight pause.*) …My brother. I have a brother. In Dublin.

             He didn't know what to do… what to do for me.

             So he paid for six sessions.

             I think he thought it might stop me trying to kill myself.

CONOR   And did it?

SUSAN   (*Looks at him.*) So far.

             Pause.

             Is that really why you're here? To kill yourself?

CONOR   I don't know.

SUSAN	You don't know much, do you?
CONOR	I'm sorry.
SUSAN	When did you get out?
CONOR	Saturday…
	Four days ago.
SUSAN	Do your family know?
CONOR	I presume so.
	The solicitor's a family friend.
SUSAN	Of course he is.
CONOR	They're good people.
	They don't deserve any of this.
SUSAN	They were quite a band in court… your mother… the brothers…!
CONOR	Good people.

Beat.

SUSAN   It's toxic.

Tragedy.

Even when you're on the right side of it.

Even when you're the victim… it sticks.

People don't get close any more. People are afraid it might catch, like fever.

I'm sure your family feel it…

Like I feel it.

He is silent.

And your wife?

Pause.

Does she know you're out?

Pause.

CONOR   I tried to see her.

SUSAN   Really?

CONOR   I tried to... I asked... the day of my release.

I love my daughter.

SUSAN   You've one hell of a way of showing it.

CONOR   Jesus...

SUSAN   Yes, 'Jesus' is right.

'Jesus' is right, Conor Bourke.

I mean what the hell do you mean by that? 'Love'?

And what the hell do you think you're doing here?!

At my café?... On my pier?... With your misery and your 'talk'?

Did I ask for this?

Did I ask for any of this?

Did Annie?

Did you think... did you ever think for a moment... about us? About me?

CONOR   I did... I do.

SUSAN   Because I really... I honestly don't care what you do to yourself. Nothing is too cruel as far as I'm concerned.

And I honestly don't care about your family or your 'love'!

I want answers. That's all.

I want to know why my daughter was in that car?

And I want to know what, in the name of God, she was doing with you...?

Pause.

CONOR   I... I... (*Sighs.*)

	JEN *enters. The lighting changes.* JEN *takes a seat. It is the past and we are in* CONOR *and* JEN*'s kitchen.* CONOR *leaves* SUSAN *and enters the scene. He is extremely agitated.*
JEN	Please, Conor, you need… we just need to stay calm.
CONOR	But I don't… I just don't know what you're saying.
JEN	It's not working.
CONOR	What's not working?
JEN	This.
	Us.
	How many ways can I say it.
	It's not working for me.
	I want to go.
	I want to try something else.
CONOR	Go?
JEN	I want to separate, Conor.
	I don't want to be married to…
	I don't want to be married.
	Long pause.
CONOR	You want to break up?
JEN	Yes. Jesus!
CONOR	Why?
JEN	Because I'm not happy.
	You're not happy.
CONOR	I am.
	I am happy.
JEN	You can't be, Conor.
	We do nothing but fight.

CONOR   We don't!

JEN   It's been bad for so long that we've forgotten…

          Forgotten what a real relationship is.

CONOR   Hold on a minute, Jen.

          I love you.

          I haven't forgotten.

          And I love Kate.

          What about Kate?

JEN   We need to leave her out of this for now.

CONOR   Leave her out of it?

          Leave Kate out of it?

JEN   She'll be better off.

CONOR   Better off how?

JEN   They say kids are better off…

CONOR   Who says?

JEN   Everyone. The experts. The books.

CONOR   What experts?

JEN   Kids are better off removed from tension.

CONOR   Removed?

JEN   You'll always be her dad.

          He gets to his feet.

CONOR   Hold on a minute.

JEN   Please stay calm.

CONOR   You no longer want to be married!

          You're leaving?

          And you think you're taking Kate?

          Not a fucking chance…

JEN   It doesn't have to be like this, Conor.

CONOR   And I'll 'always be her dad'?!

JEN   I thought… I thought we might work this out.

CONOR   I've been more of a dad than you've been mother,
           and you know that, you bitch…

JEN   I won't listen to your abuse.

           She goes to leave but he grabs her.

CONOR   Who takes her horseriding?

           Who takes her dancing?

           Who the hell is here most nights while you're out
           at your sales?

JEN   You see!

           You can't even have a conversation.

CONOR   This isn't a conversation, Jen.

           This is a fucking hijack!

           She takes a deep breath and sits down.

JEN   We are not the first couple to go through this.

CONOR   Through what exactly?

JEN   I've been to Ferriter's Solicitors.

CONOR   Oh Jesus! You are some piece of work.

           How long have you been planning this?

JEN   And they recommend…

CONOR   How long, Jen?

           Is it Ryan?

           Is he behind all this?

           Are you back screwing that fucker.

           She looks at him.

JEN   No I'm not, Conor.

           I am just trying to have a life.

           A future.

           Outside your bloody dynasty here in Athboy.

CONOR   What's that supposed to mean?

JEN   We go nowhere!

           We see no one except your family.

CONOR   What?

JEN   Every weekend, Conor... it's O'Loughlin's,
           nothing else, just sitting with your dad and your
           brothers and watching the stupid telly.

CONOR   You love O'Loughlin's.

JEN   I hate it!

           There is more to life than that bloody pub and
           your bloody shop and this bloody town.

           I've tried... I wanted... I wanted to make this work.

           I thought I loved you.

           And I think we were happy once. At the beginning.

           But I can't stand it.

           I just can't stand it now, Conor.

           And I can't stay.

CONOR   Jesus.

JEN   And it's not such a surprise to you.

           You're not stupid. I know it's not.

CONOR   But things change when you have kids...

JEN   I know they do.

           But they don't stop.

           And everything stopped for us.

CONOR   But I let you go back to work!

JEN   Did you hear that?

          Did you hear what you just said?

          You let me?

CONOR   And that was the start of it. Wasn't it?

JEN   You've always... always made that difficult for
          me.

          Everything difficult for me...

CONOR   Nothing was ever good enough for you after...

JEN   I want OUT.

          I'm sorry but I need something else.

CONOR   You need something else?

          And what about Kate?

JEN   Kate will be fine...

          If we manage this properly.

CONOR   But 'this' is her life.

          My life.

          My family

JEN   I know that...

CONOR   And she's everything to me...

          You know that, Jen.

JEN   I do. I know that.

          And that doesn't change.

CONOR   Too right it doesn't.

          You haven't told her?

          You haven't told her any of this?

          You better not have fucking told her.

JEN	Of course I haven't. We'll tell her together.
CONOR	We'll what?
JEN	There are arrangements.
	There will be arrangements.
CONOR	What kind of arrangements?
JEN	Weekends.
CONOR	You're fucking joking.
JEN	That's the way it works.
	You know that, Conor.
	And we'll do it right.
	Through the solicitor.
CONOR	You can't have her, Jen.
	No way.
	This is her home.
JEN	It can still be her home.
CONOR	What?
JEN	It can still be her home.
CONOR	On weekends?
	Pause.
JEN	Or if you move out.
CONOR	Jesus!
	Jesus Christ.
JEN	That's what people do.
	You know that that's what people do.
CONOR	You want me to go?
JEN	Not for me. I'd as happy move into one of the apartments or back to Mam. But it might be best for Kate.

CONOR   You're something else!

            Do you know that? SOME-THING else!

            So you get bored?

            Or you get laid is it?

            And it's me who has to go?

JEN   You're wrong about Ryan.

CONOR   You better hope I am.

            You better hope I am, Jen.

            Because you're right about one thing.

            I am not fucking stupid. And I can play the
            solicitor game.

            And I can get really nasty too. I'll pull you
            through every type of shite to get Kate. I won't let
            you have her.

            You might get your... your... future and your
            piss-arse career but you won't best me, Jen. You
            won't take my daughter and my house and my life.
            Be fucking warned.

            *He pushes her hard so she falls backwards off the
            chair. He stands over her. Then leaves.*

            *ANNIE enters and sits in CONOR's kitchen at the
            rented house... He hands her a plate with a
            sandwich and sits down to have one himself.*

CONOR   I let Kate have her lunch in the tent.

            Fair play to you she loves it.

ANNIE   It's just some pegs and a sheet.

CONOR   I think it's genius!

ANNIE   My mam used to let me make one behind the stairs.

            She'll be in there for hours.

            Pause... ANNIE *is delighted with herself and quite coy.*

            You cut the crusts off my sandwich!

CONOR   Is that okay?

ANNIE   Yeah.

CONOR   That's the way Kate likes hers...

ANNIE   They're lovely.

            Slight pause.

            Did you get everything you need?

            In the shop?

CONOR   Oh yeah...

            Thanks.

ANNIE   How long more will you be staying?

CONOR   I don't know exactly.

ANNIE   Why? Don't you have to work?

CONOR   Oh I do, yeah.

ANNIE   What do you work as?

CONOR   I'm in retail.

ANNIE   What's that?

CONOR   Like a shop!

ANNIE   Oh... yeah... (*Laughs.*)

            In Dublin?

CONOR   ...Yeah.

ANNIE   Is that what you did in Sydney?

CONOR   No...

ANNIE	What did you do?
CONOR	All sorts. Took tourists out fishing for a while, then sold drinks and stuff on the beach.
ANNIE	Cool.
CONOR	Yeah, I suppose it was.
	I was just there for the craic!
ANNIE	That's what I want.
	Travel.
	The craic!
	Slight pause.
CONOR	Annie…?
ANNIE	Yeah.
CONOR	Can I ask you a favour.
ANNIE	Sure.
CONOR	Now it might seem a bit strange but…
ANNIE	What?
CONOR	Would you mind not telling anyone I'm here.
ANNIE	What?
CONOR	Would you mind not telling anyone you were here today.
ANNIE	Sure I'm on the hop from school, who am I going to tell?
CONOR	I mean long-term.
ANNIE	What? Long-term?
CONOR	I mean… what I mean is… I think Kate and I might stay a bit longer but I don't really want anyone to know…
ANNIE	Why?
CONOR	Because… because her mother can be a bit tricky.

ANNIE   I thought you weren't married any more.

CONOR   And we're not. We are absolutely not. But she...
          she suffers a bit from depression.

ANNIE   Depression?

CONOR   Yeah. And she gets times when she's very down...
          unstable and it's best to keep Kate away from her
          then.

ANNIE   Wow!

CONOR   I hope you don't mind my asking.

ANNIE   No. No. Not at all. Poor Kate...

CONOR   Yes it's hard. She loves her mammy.

ANNIE   Yeah, she was telling me...

CONOR   She was?

          (*Sharp.*) What did she say?

ANNIE   Oh, I don't know... something about her mammy
          and her tea set... she likes to play with her tea set.

CONOR   Oh yes, her tea set.

ANNIE   And I think she wanted it for her tent.

CONOR   Of course and I'll get her one. I can get her one for
          here.

ANNIE   Sure you can get it in Smyths. Or I might even
          have one at home... in the box... my mam doesn't
          throw anything out.

CONOR   Aw thanks, Annie.

          He puts his hand on hers.

          I appreciate that. But it might be best not to draw
          attention...

ANNIE   Oh Jesus yeah.

CONOR   Because it's just for a couple of days... till Jen
          calms down and takes her tablets.

ANNIE	God!
	Does she get crazy?
CONOR	I'm afraid she does.
	And jealous…
	Slight pause. ANNIE *fixes her hair. She is wide-eyed.*
	I don't like Kate to see it.
ANNIE	No. Of course not.
CONOR	So can this be our secret?
	The babysitting?
	Just for the few days.
ANNIE	Sure.
	Absolutely.
CONOR	You can't even tell Claire.
ANNIE	No. No one… I promise.
CONOR	Thanks, Annie.
	You really are something else.
	He gives her a gentle hug.
	He looks at ANNIE.
	Is that her calling me?
ANNIE	Yep.
CONOR	I thought you said she'll be in there for hours!
	ANNIE *laughs. He heads back into the house. She squeezes herself, smitten.*

SUSAN   You used her.

          The lighting changes. We are back to the present.

          Didn't you?

          You just used her to keep the girl hidden.

CONOR   She asked... she asked could she come to the
          house.

          I didn't want... I swear... I had never intended...

SUSAN   Just part of your plan...

CONOR   But I didn't have a plan!

          It all just.

SUSAN   'Happened'... I know... I heard you the first time.

          Sitting in that court.

CONOR   Please...

SUSAN   And do you know what that felt like for me?

          Listening to them question her character... HER
          character... Annie!?

          They said she was a child who didn't go to school!

          A child who stayed out all night!

          A child whose mother worked... who was reared
          without a father...

          Everything... everything I thought I had achieved
          in my life. Everything I thought I was, was taken
          from me that day.

CONOR   That was wrong.

          It was all wrong.

SUSAN   Did I fail her?

          Did I really fail her?

CONOR   No.

          No... no... no...

          Susan. It was me...

> JEN *comes on stage. The lighting changes. It is the past and she is standing in* CONOR's *apartment with a plastic bag.* CONOR *leaves* SUSAN *and enters the scene.*

JEN   Hi.

CONOR   What are you doing here?

JEN   I had... I found some of your stuff.

           Your football gear.

           So I thought I'd drop it over.

CONOR   Oh okay.

           Come in.

           She enters his flat.

JEN   It's nice.

           The flat's nice.

CONOR   One of yours?

JEN   Yes.

           It was actually.

           Slight pause.

           Kate likes it.

CONOR   Did she say that?

JEN   Yeah. She did. She really likes it. She said you got her a special bed.

CONOR   It's a princess bed.

JEN   That's nice.

CONOR   I let her pick it.

JEN   Nice...

           Slight pause.

JEN   I brought you a clock.

            A present.

            I don't know if that was stupid.

CONOR   But I'm never late?!

JEN   I know. It was stupid but I just thought I should
            get you something... for the flat.

CONOR   I'm going to make it a home.

JEN   I know.

CONOR   For Kate.

JEN   I know.

CONOR   Mammy's gone mad with curtains!

JEN   I can see that.

CONOR   And she has no fucking taste.

JEN   I can see that too.

            They both laugh nervously.

            Pause.

            I just wanted to say thanks.

CONOR   For what?

JEN   Because I know it's hard.

CONOR   I think it's hard for Kate.

JEN   I know.

CONOR   She cried half the night when she was here.

JEN   That will pass.

            The doctor says it will pass.

CONOR   There's just no need for this, Jen.

            She is silent.

            I still love you.

If I've been a prick I'll stop.

I'll do anything.

JEN   It's too late.

CONOR   No it's not. It's not too late.

Because I was thinking... I was thinking, Jen,
about what you said... What you've been
saying... about us... about life.

JEN   Stop, Conor...

CONOR   No no coz... because maybe you're right. I mean
maybe I could get a new job... a new job away
from the shop, the family... and maybe we could
move... like you said... to Dublin or even go to
Dublin... to different stuff... to concerts!

JEN   Please...

CONOR   Because I'll change. I can change, Jen.

JEN   I'd like to believe that...

He moves close to her.

CONOR   Well do believe it...

JEN   No...

No, Conor... I know you... nothing changes.

CONOR   Why don't you love me?

JEN   I'm sorry...

CONOR   You're fucking killing me...

She goes to exit.

JEN   I really am... sorry...

CONOR   You care about no one but yourself.

She is gone.

CONOR *smacks his hands to his head.*

Fuck.

Then he smacks it three more times in great distress.

Fuck. Fuck. Fuck.

SUSAN   I just want to know where is she?

The lighting changes and we are back in the present.

People say the dead are with us. It's in every bereavement book. But I can't find her. When I sit at home and try to conjure... try to picture her... in bone and breath and flesh.

I can't. I walk around the house and try to smell her... try to touch something that she was the last to touch... try to call her... to dream her... but she's not there. It's like I lost her... lost her somewhere in that week... in that week she spent with you?!

The lighting changes. It is the past. CONOR stands and speaks, he is replaying a telephone conversation he had with JEN. We hear but don't see JEN... maybe with a microphone or something that distorts her. CONOR speaks very calmly, almost like he is in a trance.

CONOR   Hello... Jen?

JEN   Conor?

CONOR   Yeah it's me.

JEN   Sweet Jesus.

         Where are you?

         I've been worried sick.

CONOR   I'm fine.

JEN   Where's Kate?

CONOR   She's with me.

          She's fine.

JEN   You were supposed to drop her back last night.

CONOR   I know.

JEN   And you haven't answered your phone.

CONOR   I forgot the charger.

JEN   Where are you?

          I rang your mother and she doesn't know?

CONOR   I just… we just went away for a few days.

          I thought it would be nice.

JEN   You went away?

CONOR   Yes.

JEN   Where?

CONOR   It was spur-of-the-moment.

JEN   Well you better get back here right now.

          Put Kate on the phone.

          I want to talk to her.

CONOR   Kate's at the house.

JEN   What house?

          Where are you?

CONOR   It doesn't matter.

          I want…

          I think we'll stay for the rest of the week.

JEN   Are you fucking joking?!

CONOR   It's not working, Jen.

JEN   What's... what's not working?

CONOR   The arrangements.

            They're not working for me.

            I want us to try something else.

JEN   Please. Just put Kate on the phone, Conor.

            I want to talk to her.

CONOR   I'm afraid I won't do that.

JEN   What?

CONOR   It might unsettle her.

            She's fine.

            She's enjoying herself.

JEN   What?... How?... Conor... Conor, listen to me.

            She needs to be back at school. Kate needs... and
            we can look at things... Look! – we can look at
            everything.

CONOR   Yeah. That's good, that sounds good, Jen.

JEN   But you need to come home.

CONOR   And we will. We will when we're ready.

            *He hangs up. He sits, contemplating the call. He is
            extremely calm. We hear* JEN, *she is frantic...*

JEN   Conor. Conor!

            He smiles.

ANNIE comes on stage. The lighting changes. It is the past and ANNIE is on the couch at CONOR's rented house. CONOR enters.

ANNIE   Hiya!

CONOR   Hi. How is everything?

ANNIE   Great… everything's great. I'm just watching telly.

CONOR   Good woman…

ANNIE   Kate went to bed easy.

           She loves those new books you bought her.

CONOR   Yes she does.

ANNIE   So how did that go?

CONOR   How did what go?

ANNIE   Your telephone call?

CONOR   Good good.

ANNIE   Is she okay?

           Did she take her tablets?

CONOR   Yeah… but she needs a rest. She's taking a rest. So she doesn't want us back for a while. I'm afraid she's really not well.

ANNIE   Oh…

CONOR   But I don't want to tell Kate.

           We'll just say it's an extended holiday.

ANNIE   Of course.

           …It must be really tough…

CONOR   Ah, it's alright.

           What's important is to protect Kate.

ANNIE   She's lucky to have you…

           He smiles and puts his hand on hers.

CONOR   And I appreciate your help, Annie.

          I don't know how I could manage without you.

          She leans in and then tries to kiss him.

          Hey... Hey... Hey...

          She jumps up.

ANNIE   Sorry!

CONOR   No...

ANNIE   I'm sorry, that was stupid.

CONOR   No...

ANNIE   No one ever wants me.

          She goes to leave.

CONOR   Hang on... what's this?

ANNIE   No one ever wants me... that way...

CONOR   But you're beautiful.

ANNIE   I'm not. I'm dog-ugly.

          He holds her by the shoulders.

CONOR   Hey... hey, hey. I said: YOU'RE BEAUTIFUL.

          I'm just way... way too old for you.

ANNIE   I don't think you are.

CONOR   Annie, you're a terrific girl... and you're anything
          but ugly... but I'm, Jesus... my life is way too
          complicated right now. I can't... I couldn't get
          involved... not till I sort this out with Jen...
          maybe get full custody... I'm just not a free
          agent... I couldn't... even if I wanted to...

          Pause.

ANNIE   Does that mean you want to?

          He strokes her face with his hand.

CONOR   That means: don't go. It's lonely here without you.

ANNIE   Lonely?

CONOR   Yeah.

           And I got us some pizza.

           You love pizza, right?

           Half-laughs.

ANNIE   I do. I love pizza.

CONOR   And we can watch a movie.

           Stay for a bit.

           Okay?

ANNIE   Okay…

           The lighting changes and CONOR *talks to*
           SUSAN *in the present.*

CONOR   I wish to God I could turn back the clock. Stop it.
           Stop it all from spinning… just spinning away… I
           play it. I play it over and over in my head. That
           Friday I collected Kate from school. I play it so it
           has a different ending. I play it so I put her bag
           and coat in the boot and we talk about her new
           reader… what she did at breaktime… and then we
           go to the Village Kitchen for some cake… or we
           go to my mother's and she plays in the garden…
           or we go to the park… we go… anywhere…
           anywhere but here.

SUSAN   Anywhere but here…

CONOR   I wasn't myself… I know that sounds pathetic… I
           know that sounds just like a cliché, another
           excuse. But the truth is I don't know… I just don't
           know what happened to me… how I lost it… how
           I lost my grip…

           Pause.

           All I could think of was Jen – what a bitch she
           was!… What a conniving betraying bitch… and

how she held those reins... how she held them. So
tight, so tight... like her tight little arse walking
around my house... walking away with my life.

*JEN enters. The lighting changes and we are in
the past. JEN is coming out of her house early
morning. CONOR is in the garden.*

CONOR   Where's Kate?

JEN   Conor?

CONOR   Where is she?

JEN   What are you doing here?

CONOR   You never came home yesterday.

JEN   What?

CONOR   When you collected Kate from school.

    You didn't come back here.

JEN   We went to my mother's.

CONOR   So where is she now?

JEN   She's at my mother's!

CONOR   And your mother is driving her to school?

JEN   Sorry, Conor, what the fuck are you doing here?

CONOR   Your mother is an atrocious driver.

JEN   It's eight o'clock in the morning!

CONOR   I'm entitled to know where my daughter sleeps.

JEN   This is unbelievable.

    You are unbelievable, Conor.

    Slight pause.

    Have you been hanging around the school?

CONOR   What?

JEN   How did you know about yesterday?

CONOR   ...I was driving by.

JEN   Since when do you drive by the school, Conor?

CONOR   Sometimes I do.

JEN   Jesus Christ.

          She was right.

CONOR   Who was right?

JEN   Kate.

          She says she sees you sometimes at the gates.

          But I thought... I hoped she was imagining it.

CONOR   I wasn't by the gates.

JEN   You've been hanging around the school!

CONOR   You didn't give her any lunch on Monday.

          I had to drive down to Centra to buy her a
          sandwich.

JEN   Jesus.

          What's got into you?

          You can just ask if you want to see her...

CONOR   ASK?

          ASK, Jen! To see my own daughter.

JEN   Like I ASK when she's got her time with you.

CONOR   So where were you last night?

JEN   What?

CONOR   Where were you?

          Why did you have to dump Kate?

JEN   I didn't dump Kate.

I went to a gig in Dublin.

And Mammy wanted to have her for the night.

CONOR   You should have asked me.

JEN   Why?

CONOR   You need my permission.

JEN   I don't.

CONOR   Well I'm recording it.

JEN   You're what?

CONOR   I'm recording everything, Jen, because I know you'll fuck up.

JEN   Go home, Conor.

Get the hell out of my garden and let me go to work.

CONOR   This is my garden.

JEN   Oh Christ...

CONOR   And they are my gates so don't think you can change the code.

JEN   I have no intention of changing the code, what's got into you?

CONOR   I can get in to this house any time I like.

Pause.

JEN   This isn't normal, Conor.

The way you are. The way you are being.

It isn't normal.

CONOR   I don't like the way you're managing Kate.

JEN   There are arrangements.

We made an agreement.

We stick to the agreement.

CONOR   And dumping her at your mother's is part of that?!

JEN   I am going to work.

CONOR   So she won't see a parent for nearly twenty-four hours.

            I wonder how your solicitor will feel about that?

JEN   My solicitor has more important things to worry about.

CONOR   Well there's nothing more important to me than Kate.

            That's the difference between you and ME, Jen.

JEN   I'm serious, Conor.

            I am beginning to worry about you.

            This behaviour… you should talk to someone.

CONOR   You don't give a shit about me.

JEN   I do actually.

            I do.

            Pause.

            I heard about the shop.

CONOR   What? What did you hear?

JEN   That the receivers are in.

CONOR   This fucking town… it's nothing but talk…

JEN   I know you're under pressure.

            Your family are under pressure.

CONOR   I am not under any pressure.

JEN   Do you want to reduce the maintenance? I'm still doing well…

CONOR   Fuck off.

            I can look after my own daughter.

JEN   Okay.

            This is obviously useless.

CONOR   It's you who is useless, Jen.

JEN   Please go home, Conor.

CONOR   No I'm going to the school.

          Kate doesn't like to be late.

JEN   She won't be late.

          Mammy's dropping her.

          You can't keep showing up at the school.

CONOR   Someone's got to keep an eye on this.

JEN   On what?

CONOR   On you.

JEN   You're starting to make me nervous.

CONOR   Good.

JEN   You need to get on with your own life!

CONOR   But Kate is my life, Jen.

JEN   God!

          Just listen to yourself, will you, Conor?

          And look at yourself. None of this is normal.

CONOR   I don't take advice from you...

JEN   Okay.

          Okay then.

          I'm going to work.

CONOR   I'll be over Friday.

JEN   Fine.

CONOR   She's mine on Friday...

The lighting changes and we are back to the present. CONOR *talks to* SUSAN.

CONOR   I couldn't face that flat.

I couldn't face that failure…

I remember looking back.

Back into the back seat through the mirror.

And seeing Kate.

And she smiled at me.

In her new coat.

A new coat I had no part in.

A new coat I didn't buy.

So I didn't stop. I couldn't stop.

I wouldn't take my weekend.

My allocation.

I'd show that bitch.

I'd show them all.

I drove on.

SUSAN   To here.

CONOR   To here.

SUSAN   And that day.

The last day.

JEN *comes on stage now as the two stories merge.*
The lights focus on her and CONOR *enters the*
space.

CONOR   Hello, Jen.

JEN   I thought I'd never have to see you again.

CONOR   Thanks. Thank you so much for agreeing to this…

Pause.

JEN   I agreed, Conor. I agreed so that I could say one
thing to you. Just one thing and then I'm gone.

I will never bring Kate to you… so don't ask. Not
ever. And don't ask the social workers… because I
promised myself… I promised myself something
on that pier… I promised that if they brought her
out alive… if they lifted Kate from that freezing
water… I would never, EVER let you within a
hair's breadth of her again.

Lights spin to SUSAN.

SUSAN   Why did Annie go to you?

Why did she lie?

CONOR   She was… she came around every day… after
school… or into the evening. And she'd watch
Kate…

SUSAN   She said she was babysitting…

CONOR   And she was… You see! She was… because it
was getting risky… I couldn't take Kate out any
more… I just knew Jen would contact the police
after the call… I knew she'd come looking.

JEN speaks and the light spins to her.

JEN   If you have a shred of decency left in you, you
will leave us alone.

She makes to exit.

CONOR   Please… don't go, Jen…

You can't go...

I have rights.

She turns to look at him.

JEN   Do you?

Do you really think you do?

Even after you tried to kill her?

CONOR   Don't say that... how can you say that...?

That's not...

That's not what I wanted, Jen, and you know it.

I love her.

JEN   What you did.

What you tried to do to us, Conor.

That has nothing to do with love.

Beat.

CONOR   Does she ask for me?

Does Kate ever ask for me?

JEN   No.

Never.

She exits.

The light spins back to SUSAN.

SUSAN   But why was she there that morning?

CONOR   I don't know!

SUSAN   You told her to come over?

CONOR   I didn't...

I didn't know that they had found me.

Slight pause.

SUSAN   I go over it all again too. I play it in my head just like you described... but I can't change the ending.

I don't know what I could have done differently?

I don't know what I could have said that morning?

That might have stopped her.

Slight pause.

And it's the most... it's the most meaningless memory... a rushed conversation... not even a conversation...

ANNIE *now comes on stage but stands separate to* SUSAN.

Have you got your coat on, love?

ANNIE   *I don't need it, Mam.*

SUSAN   *Yes you do, you need it for school. I heard you sniffling through the night... and it's gone cold again.*

ANNIE   *But I hate the coat. It looks ridiculous.*

SUSAN   *You know it's too cold to be without your coat, Annie.*

ANNIE   *Arghh okay, Mam.*

SUSAN   *Good girl...*

ANNIE   *See ya!*

SUSAN   *See ya!*

And that was it.

That was the last time I ever spoke to her.

And I didn't even turn around.

I had my head in the sink.

I didn't even look at her.

On our last morning.

She struggles with her emotions.

But then she didn't go to school.

She didn't go to school, did she? She went to you.

The light spins to ANNIE. *It is the past. She is arriving at* CONOR*'s rented house.*

ANNIE Hey!

CONOR Annie...!

He is pumping... anxious.

ANNIE I couldn't stand the thought of school...

CONOR Okay, come in... come in.

ANNIE What's up?

CONOR Don't hang around the door, just come in will you.

ANNIE Jesus what's up?

CONOR Actually it's good you're here.

Yes it's good you're here.

ANNIE Is it?

CONOR I need you.

I'll need you.

ANNIE Why, what's wrong?

Where's Kate?

CONOR She's inside. She's just inside.

But don't go in yet!

ANNIE Why?

CONOR She's alright, she's watching TV and I'm thinking... I've got to plan... I've got to think.

ANNIE Think about what?

CONOR There's something going on.

ANNIE What's going on?

CONOR I think we will have to go away.

ANNIE Who?

CONOR Me and Kate.

	Me and Kate, Annie, because the police were around.
ANNIE	The police?
CONOR	Just minutes ago.
	Gards... the Gards.
ANNIE	But what did they want?
CONOR	I think they're looking for Kate.
ANNIE	But why?
CONOR	They were asking questions.
	Lots of questions.
ANNIE	But you're her dad?
CONOR	I know.
	I think it's because I rang Jen.
	I shouldn't have rang Jen.
	She's probably twisted it. She twists everything Annie... all the time...
ANNIE	But Jen is off her head!
	They must know that.
CONOR	That doesn't seem to matter.
	We'll just have to go.
ANNIE	Go where?
CONOR	England!
	We'll go to England.
ANNIE	I don't want you to go to England!
CONOR	I have no choice.
ANNIE	But tell them. Just tell them that she's crazy. Kate's better off with you. I don't understand this.
CONOR	They won't listen.

They don't listen, Annie... she has them all in her pocket...

...the Gards... the teachers... the solicitors...

I've been through this all before.

ANNIE   Okay.

So I'll come too...

CONOR   No...

ANNIE   I'll have to... how else will you manage?

CONOR   I'll manage...

ANNIE   But you have to get money, don't you?

If we are going to go to England.

And we'll have to pack up the car.

Is there petrol?

CONOR   You're right.

I'm not prepared.

What a fucking fool.

I'm not prepared...

ANNIE   But I can help, Conor.

I can pack up... and watch Kate.

So you can go and get everything else.

CONOR   Good girl.

You're right, Annie

You're right.

ANNIE   And I won't say anything to her.

I'll keep her playing.

We'll explain when you get back.

CONOR   Okay...

ANNIE   Okay.

CONOR   You're amazing. You know that.

*He hugs her and she kisses him. She is passionate
so he kisses her back. Then he quickly pulls away.*

Don't go outside?

ANNIE   Don't worry.

CONOR   And don't call anyone?

ANNIE   I won't.

CONOR   It's just you and me and Kate.

ANNIE   I know.

She kisses him again. She is high with excitement.

I love you.

CONOR *leaves.*

The light spins back to SUSAN

SUSAN   And it was such a beautiful morning. One of those
rare spring mornings when it's cold but the sun is
out and splitting the stones.

That's why I was stood at the window... looking
out here onto the pier. I was taking it all in – the
sunshine – the morning.

But then I saw you... I saw your car.

The light spins back to ANNIE.

ANNIE   Conor! Conor.

CONOR   What?

ANNIE   They were back.

The Gards.

And they were looking around the house.

CONOR   So what did you say?

ANNIE   I didn't open the door.

We pretended the house was empty... me and Kate...

I let on it was a game... hide and seek.

CONOR   Good girl.

ANNIE   I've everything ready.

Come on!

The light spins back to SUSAN.

SUSAN   Your car was on the pier.

And there was Annie.

There was Annie in the front seat.

Why isn't she in school?

That was my first thought. Jesus, when I think of it.

You see I could see her hair, her ponytail, and it was flicking across her face when she looked out of the window... when you reversed.

It flicked across her face like it's done since she was a child.

'Why isn't she in school?!'

You'd think I'd be more alarmed by the speed of the car.

You'd think I'd be more alarmed by the sound of the police.

But there was such consternation!

Consternation on the pier.

The cars. The sirens.

And I just couldn't figure... how was Annie?

What was Annie doing in the middle of all this?

CONOR   I swear... I told her not to... I told her not to get into the car.

I told her I didn't, I could never love her.

I told her to go home.

But as I was buckling in Kate.

She locked the passenger door...

And there was just no time...

There was no time...

I knew the police were coming...

SUSAN   She might have caught sight of me.

Did she?

I so hope to God she did... as you screeched backwards toward my window. Turning the car toward the sea. I could see your little girl. I could see her head pop over the child seat. And the flick of Annie's hair... as you lurched forward...

The light spins to ANNIE *who screams.*

ANNIE   Conor!

What are you doing?

What are you doing?

We can't reach the road this way.

CONOR   Okay... okay... don't worry, Daddy's going to fix this, Katie.

ANNIE   Please... please... we have to stop.

You have to stop the car right now...

The light stops on CONOR.

CONOR   And that was the only thing I could think of. The only thing I could do. To stop it. To just stop it all dead.

And it seemed so clear. So perfect in that moment.

Like it was such a simple solution.

For me and for Kate.

Where we could be happy again.

We could be finished with all this.

We hear ANNIE *scream.*

So I slammed my foot to the pedal. Slammed it down and drove on.

SUSAN   On and into the sea.

Pause.

But what about Annie?

He looks at SUSAN.

Did you even think about Annie?

In that moment. Your perfect moment.

CONOR   No.

SUSAN   You didn't care.

Slight pause.

CONOR   I didn't care.

Silence.

SUSAN   (*Quietly.*) You never said that in court!

He hangs his head.

Pause.

Tell me what happened to her?

…as you sped towards the water?

CONOR   I don't… I don't remember…

SUSAN   Please!

Slight pause.

CONOR   She tried to get out…

SUSAN   Yes.

They said she was out of her seatbelt.

CONOR   She screamed and begged me to stop.

SUSAN   Of course she did.

CONOR   But it was too late.

SUSAN   You hit the water.

CONOR   We hit the water.

          And it was a crash.

          It was violent.

          And I think that Annie was thrown.

SUSAN   They said she hit her head.

CONOR   Yes she hit her head.

SUSAN   Then that means she was unconscious. Was she?

          She didn't know... she didn't know that she might drown.

CONOR   I don't know...

SUSAN   She wasn't frightened... it happened fast and the last thing she saw... maybe the last thing she saw... was me.

          Me looking out through this window...

          Wondering why she wasn't in school.

CONOR   Yes.

          She was.

          She was unconscious.

          She hit her head.

          I remember now.

          She hit her head just after she called your name.

          SUSAN *grabs on to this*.

SUSAN   She called my name...?!

CONOR   Yes.

SUSAN   How?

CONOR   Mam… she called Mam… Mammy.

SUSAN   Did she?

CONOR   Yes.

She called you.

She saw you.

Standing in the window.

You were with her, Susan.

You were with her as we hit the water.

Like you were with her…

SUSAN   All her life.

CONOR   All her life.

SUSAN sees ANNIE now. She reaches out her hand to her. She whispers.

SUSAN   Annie.

ANNIE smiles at SUSAN.

Thank you.

Thank you, Conor Bourke.

Slight pause.

CONOR   I tried to help them save her. The hands in the water, Susan. The Gards. Kate's window was open… that's how they pulled us out. But Annie… I tried… I lifted… I pulled… but she was a deadweight… all that gave was the locket… your locket and then the water… it was crushing… it… I… She.

Fuck… I'm sorry… I'm so sorry.

Pause.

SUSAN slowly stands up from the chair. She opens the door of the café to enter… then turns.

SUSAN   You've caused so much pain already… you know that.

And if you do it – if you drown and they find you... out there in the ocean. That will only make life worse...

For Jen... and for Kate.

Do you really still want to hurt them?

He looks at her.

CONOR   She said there's no going back?

SUSAN   No.

There's no going back.

Slight pause.

CONOR   But what will you do?

SUSAN   I don't know.

Maybe it's time to go.

And start something... start something... somewhere else.

Slight pause. Then she closes the door of the café.

CONOR *is alone... He looks toward the sea... We can hear the sea.*

SUSAN *stands in the window watching him.*

He walks down towards the water. He hesitates.

Then he digs his hands down into his pockets. He turns away from the sea and exits.

SUSAN *stands in the window just as she did at the beginning of the play.*

The lights fade.

End.

A Nick Hern Book

Spinning first published in Great Britain in 2014 as a paperback original by Nick Hern Books Limited, The Glasshouse, 49a Goldhawk Road, London W12 8QP, in association with Fishamble: The New Play Company

Spinning copyright © 2014 Deirdre Kinahan

Deirdre Kinahan has asserted her moral right to be identified as the author of this work

Cover photograph by Leo Byrne

Designed and typeset by Nick Hern Books, London
Printed in Great Britain by CPI Group (UK) Ltd

A CIP catalogue record for this book is available from the British Library

ISBN 978 1 84842 431 9